GUIDELINES FOR RESPONSIBLE DRINKING

GUIDELINES FOR RESPONSIBLE DRINKING

By

GARY G. FORREST, ED.D., PH.D.

Clinical Psychologist and Executive Director
Psychotherapy Associates, P.C., and
The Institute for Addictive Behavioral Change
Colorado Springs, Colorado

JASON ARONSON INC.
Northvale, New Jersey
London

THE MASTER WORK SERIES

First softcover edition 1994

Library of Congress Cataloging-in-Publication Data

Forrest, Gary G.
Guidelines for responsible drinking / by Gary G. Forrest.
p. cm.
Originally published: Springfield, Ill. : C.C. Thomas, c1989.
Includes bibliographical references and index.
ISBN 1-56821-430-8
1. Drinking of alcoholic beverages—United States. 2. Drinking of alcoholic beverages—Social aspects—United States.
3. Entertaining—United States. I. Title.
HV5292.F67 1995
394.1'3—dc20 94-40569

Manufactured in the United States of America. Jason Aronson Inc. offers books and cassettes. For information and catalog write to Jason Aronson Inc., 230 Livingston Street, Northvale, New Jersey 07647.

To Boog, Bud, and Stid—The Whole Crew, and especially Flossie Forrest-Summy—a bona fide responsible drinker for over fifty years!

FOREWORD

You may think it odd or even "betraying" that a recovering alcoholic would have *anything* to do with a book on responsible drinking! However, you need to remember that we recovering people represent a *minority* of the adult population. That is, *most* people in this country do *not* have a problem with drinking alcohol.

This is *not* a book for active alcoholics, looking for a "way out" of their problem, nor for any of the population that may have been diagnosed by competent professionals as having a drinking problem or just even "being in trouble" with alcohol.

What may be happening is that you do not have any tools to help you with *responsible* use of alcohol. You can't or don't handle so-called social drinking, host or hostess duties and pressures, or just the kind of social "mixers" that may include alcohol on the agenda.

When I wrote *The Joy Of Being Sober,* I was and *am* addressing the alcoholics and the need to find other ways to lead a joyful, happy and full life *without* using alcohol. I can *never* return to social drinking, nor can any other diagnosed alcoholic. My life has changed so that even if it were possible by some "magic cure" for me to drink alcohol again, I would not do so.

This, like all ordered processes in life, is a *chosen* behavior for me! We know that alcohol, in moderate use, can be a relaxer of tensions, an agent that helps relieve anxiety temporarily, and may, when used in moderation, be an aid to overcoming many of the behavior complexities that plague some human beings.

Doctor Forrest has skillfully addressed the needs of this *latter* population and the methods and ways that alcohol can be *responsibly* handled by the non-alcoholic, social drinker.

My personal great respect for Gary Forrest and his clinical knowledge and ability has been nurtured over the years as more and more of his research and writings have become published and, thus, available to all of us in the professional treatment field.

His material has formed many cornerstones for those of us who deal on a professional level with alcoholics and their families, and his clinical practice continues to reflect his standing among his peers.

Responsible use of alcohol is as much a right for the *non-alcoholic* person as responsible use of firearms or operation of an automobile is for the *non-criminal* persons in our society.

Moderation in *all* things continues to be a watchword, and this book can help underscore that life-style.

—Jack Mumey, Author of:
The Joy Of Being Sober
Loving An Alcoholic
Young Alcoholics, A Book For Parents
Good Food For A Sober Life (with Anne Hatcher)

PREFACE

This book is about responsible drinking and responsible alcohol use. Most of us have wondered about or questioned the drinking behaviors of a close friend or family member. Perhaps you have even asked yourself "Am I a responsible drinker?" The fact is that the vast majority of people, including behavioral scientists and even alcohol counselors, do not know what constitutes responsible alcohol use. All too frequently, we serve alcoholic beverages at parties and socialize with alcohol, but deep down inside we wonder if we are doing the "right thing." Can people entertain and socialize responsibly with alcohol? Some people believe that any alcohol use is irresponsible.

Each chapter in this book explores the concept of responsible drinking within a different social context: the family and between parents and children, social events and entertaining, intimate and sexual relationships, the world of work, driving automobiles, with other mood-altering drugs, and so forth. The beliefs and attitudes surrounding the matter of responsible drinking are diverse, confusing, and emotionally charged. Hopefully, the content of this book will help you better understand the responsible-irresponsible dimensions of your own alcohol use as well as those of significant others with whom you are involved.

Finally, a word of caution: This book is not written for alcoholics or anyone with a severe drinking problem. There are no guidelines in this book that will somehow magically help alcoholics and alcohol abusers become responsible drinkers. It is the author's opinion that alcoholism is a disorder or disease that preludes the possibility of responsible alcohol use. As such, this book is not recommended reading for drinking alcoholics, alcohol abusers, or other "practicing" addicts and substance abusers.

Gary G. Forrest

CONTENTS

GUIDELINES FOR RESPONSIBLE DRINKING

Chapter 1

INTRODUCTION

I have spent sixteen years working with alcoholics, problem drinkers, substance abusers, and their families and loved ones. My entire professional career has been devoted to the treatment and understanding of people who manifest drinking disorders and other addictions. Like the vast majority of health professionals involved in this field, my therapeutic and educational efforts have been directed toward the goal of helping alcoholics and alcohol abusers stop drinking. My clinical experiences with alcoholics and addicts over these sixteen years have taught me a great deal. One very basic and simple thing that I have learned through my experiences with over two thousand alcoholic patients is that these individuals, for whatever reason or reasons, are unable to drink responsibly! They are simply unable to consistently control their drinking once they have ingested ethanol. Indeed, a major common denominator that all alcoholics share is simply the inability to control their drinking. Alcoholics *are unable* to drink responsibly!

Unfortunately, health professionals and treatment personnel such as myself are usually so involved in the various processes of treating alcoholics and problem drinkers that we tend to overlook or lose sight of the fact that most people are responsible drinkers! The vast majority of drinkers are not alcoholics or consistent alcohol abusers. Less than 20 percent of drinkers in America are alcoholics and problem drinkers. We know that about 10 percent of drinkers in this country develop alcoholism or a very serious drinking disorder. Approximately 20 percent of our adult population are non-drinkers.

Health professionals that work with alcoholics, addicts, and substance abusers are understandably most concerned about teaching their patients to recover through alcohol and drug abstinence. Health professionals in the addiction's treatment field do not really talk about "responsible drinking." We have not addressed the various issues that are associated with the reality that most drinkers are indeed responsible drinkers! There is very little, if any, literature available in the alcoholism field that outlines or explores the concept of responsible drinking. It is not surprising that recovering alcoholics and their spouses and family members are uninterested in the concept of responsible drinking. Recovering individuals and their family members have usually had the very painful experience of "rediscovering" on hundreds of occasions that they were unable to drink responsibly! The Alcoholics Anonymous community (AA, Al-Anon, Ala-Teen, and Ala-Tot) is also generally uninterested in the concept of responsible drinking, as this group is made up exclusively of people who have been devastated by the effects of irresponsible and uncontrollable drinking.

I have observed over the years that physicians and behavioral scientists in general tend to underdiagnose or misdiagnose alcoholism and alcohol abuse. To the contrary, recovering health professionals and people involved in the alcoholism and addiction treatment field tend to overdiagnose alcoholics and alcohol abuse. I have also long suspected that most of us in the alcoholism field have avoided discussing the issue of "responsible drinking" for a number of political and even economic reasons. Behavioral scientists as well as the general public recognize that most people are not alcohol dependent or alcohol abusers. Yet, all of us tend to preconsciously fear that we will promote or reinforce alcohol abuse and addiction vis-à-vis any widespread discussion and elucidation of the concept of responsible drinking.

Alcoholism researchers and clinicians, as well as the public, also equate the concept of responsible drinking with the matter of *controlled* drinking. The alcoholism field has never satisfactorily resolved the question of controlled drinking, and it seems as though this issue continually raises its head. Alcoholism researchers have consistently found that a small percentage of treated alcoholics are able to "control" their drinking after treatment. As I have discussed over the years, there are actually many different "kinds" or subgroups of alcoholics, and it is not particularly surprising in a statistical sense to find that some of these treated "alcoholics" return to a pattern of non-addictive, non-problematic consumption. By the same token, many alcoholics as well as non-alcoholic drinkers simply stop drinking as a result of both treatment and no treatment. However, let me point out that I have not treated a single primary alcoholic patient in sixteen years of clinical practice that has been able to successfully control his or her drinking behavior for an extended period of time. Invariably, these individuals relapse into a pattern of extremely destructive, irresponsible, and uncontrolled consumption.

These issues are all associated with our historic reluctance to explore the concept of responsible drinking. Treatment program directors, alcoholism counselors and therapists, and hospital administrators associate the concept of responsible drinking with the controversial issue of controlled drinking. Treatment programs and behavioral scientists that have advocated controlled drinking have been the recipients of scathing attacks and even lawsuits by their professional colleagues, former patients, and the media. Most alcohol treatment facilities will not employ counselors who advocate controlled drinking approaches. Federal agencies are reluctant to fund research projects and agencies that promote the goal of controlled drinking. Most community leaders are reluctant to support community agencies as well as private alcoholism treatment agencies that provide treatments aimed at helping alcoholics and alcohol abusers become social or controlled drinkers.

It is important for the reader to bear in mind that responsible drinking may or may not be linked to the issue of controlled drinking. Obviously, a responsible drinker is in control of his or her use of alcohol. In this sense, controlled drinking is responsible drinking. Yet, I want you to clearly understand from the outset of this book that there are no guidelines in these pages that will enable or teach alcoholics and severe alcohol abusers how to drink alcohol responsibly! My cogent message to you in this regard is that alcoholics cannot drink responsibly, during, after, or in the absence of treatment. Many of these individuals were unable to drink responsibly the first time they ingested an alcoholic beverage!

The picture is really quite clear. Most people are drinkers who drink responsibly. Yet, most of us—parents, adolescents, physicians, educators, and even counselors and therapists—that "treat" alcoholics and alcohol abusers are not sure what "responsible drinking" means or entails. For some individuals responsible drinking seems to be an impossibility. A few people may believe that there is no such thing as responsible drinking under any circumstances. Alcohol and drug educators have been reluctant and perhaps afraid to explore the concept of responsible drinking. I certainly understand and appreciate all of the realities. God only knows how many lives and families are destroyed each day as a function of irresponsible drinking. Yet, I do not believe that an examination of the nature of responsible drinking will in any way reinforce the incidence of alcoholism or alcohol abuse in any society. In fact, I feel that it is time for those of us in the alcoholism and addiction's field to direct our research and investigative efforts toward non-pathological drinkers and patterns of non-abusive consumption.

Until recently, we have focused almost exclusively upon the treatment of alcoholics, spouses, children, and families of alcoholics, and adult children of alcoholics. We have investigated or begun to study most of the deviant or pathological facets of alcoholism and alcohol abuse. Perhaps we can ultimately learn a great deal more about the susceptibility to alcoholism, early identification of alcoholics and abusers, and prevention of alcoholism by investigating and better understanding non-alcoholic and non-abusive patterns of alcohol consumption. Such an undertaking must be based upon a clear understanding of normative or responsible drinking. In the evolution of the behavioral sciences we seem to progress from investigations that deal with pathology, illness, and aberrant or deviant conditions to studies of health, well-being, and optimal adjustment. It is simply time for alcoholism researchers and clinicians to initiate more comprehensive and better-designed studies that pertain to the matters of responsible and non-pathological patterns of alcohol consumption. We need to begin to systematically and comprehensively investigate the drinking behaviors and drinking patterns of responsible drinkers.

As I lecture and provide alcoholism consultation services throughout the United States the "question" of responsible drinking seems to come up over and over again. Parents want to know if the drinking behavior of a son or daughter is "normal." When is too much, too much? Spouses and children of alcoholics often ask if there really is such a "thing" as responsible drinking. Even medical doctors, psychologists, and alcoholism counselors, and the so-called "experts" consistently ask me questions that are associated with the issue of responsible drinking. The experts are often perplexed about the nature of responsible drinking. Many social drinkers wonder from time to time if they are drinking too much.

Guidelines for Responsible Drinking is the result of a ferment within me that has been created by these very questions in combination with my clinical work in the alcoholism and addiction's field. In this book I have explored the basic concepts of responsibility and responsible living and then applied these concepts to a diversity of situations that frequently involve drinking and alcohol consumption. Parental drinking behaviors, adolescent alcohol use, drinking and driving, socializing and entertaining, alcohol in the world of work, alcohol and drugs, alcohol and sex, and alcoholism and alcohol abuse are topics that are discussed in this book.

Rather specific guidelines and parameters are provided for the responsible as well as irresponsible use of alcohol in each of these social and situational contexts.

The subject matter of this book is also complex and perhaps confusing. For example, it can be relatively easy for the experienced alcohol counselor to diagnose and assess alcoholism or problem drinking. However, it may be very difficult for a counselor or family member to delineate guidelines for the responsible use of alcoholic beverages at a family social gathering! This book does provide the reader with guidelines for responsible alcohol use in a variety of different and sometimes confusing social contexts. The content of this book will also make the reader evaluate and perhaps reevaluate many of his or her beliefs and assumptions about alcohol use. I think it will be important for the reader to view this book as a beginning point in our attempts to better understand the different aspects of responsible drinking.

Chapter 2

DEFINING AND UNDERSTANDING RESPONSIBLE BEHAVIOR

BASIC BELIEFS, DEFINITIONS, AND CONCEPTS

Any behavior or act may in some manner reflect a sense of responsibility or irresponsibility. Indeed, there are shades or gradients of responsibility associated with all of our human interactions and behaviors. The concept of responsible behavior is intricately interwoven with every facet and dimension of our daily lives. Think about this for a moment. When we stop at a red light in our vehicle we expect the driver behind us to be attentive and responsible. Thus, we also expect him to stop for the red light. If he is not attentive, driving under the influence of alcohol or other drugs, or angry and in a hurry, he may not drive his vehicle responsibly. In fact, his irresponsible driving may cause us to be involved in an automobile accident or even lose our life!

In the business world we are totally dependent upon telephones. Responsible businessmen make it a point to promptly return their phone calls. Consider what your business world might be like if all of a sudden you stopped returning calls or if your business colleagues stopped returning your calls. We expect our husbands, wives and children to behave responsibly and tell us where they are going, what they are doing, when to expect them to return, and so forth. Our lives are organized and centered around the concept of responsibility.

There are several factors that can confuse or distort our understanding of responsible behavior. First of all, we do not always agree with each other about the nature or dimensions of responsible behavior. I may perceive a behavior or act as highly responsible in nature while you may believe that this same act is somewhat irresponsible or grossly irresponsible. Furthermore, there are individual, family, social, and collective realities that shape our beliefs and perceptions about responsible behavior. Consider our current struggle with Libya. Is it only a small segment of

Libyan and Iranian terrorists that believe it is appropriate, justified, and responsible to blow up airplanes and kill innocent children? Perhaps most Libyans perceive these behaviors and acts as responsible? Yet, the vast majority of American's and European's perceive these acts as completely irresponsible and senseless. We see these irresponsible behaviors as the acts of "madmen," "psychotics," and "cowards." The confusing fact is that individual, family, community, legal, social and collective norms shape and influence our attitudes about responsible behavior. There is also a tremendous amount of variance within families, individuals, and cultures relative to beliefs and definitions of responsible behavior. Laws, social rules and norms are always evolving.

Consider the confusion, change, and variance in our beliefs in the United States that surround the issue of responsible sexual behavior. Before the birth control pill and other effective contraceptive methods were developed it was generally considered irresponsible for a man to impregnate his fiancée or girl friend. Is the act of impregnation when the girl friend is taking birth control pills perceived as less irresponsible today? Homosexual relationships were generally believed to be pathologic and irresponsible forty or fifty years ago in the United States and most Western cultures. Fifteen or twenty years ago the "between consenting adults" belief system made homosexual relationships more acceptable and the importance of responsible and healthy relationships between homosexuals was emphasized. Today, we have AIDS. How do we define responsible sexual interactions between mutually consenting homosexual men and women when these relationships may result in widespread illness and death?

There are many difficulties associated with defining and clearly understanding the concept of responsible behavior. However, most people do have a relatively structured and internalized set of standards by which they evaluate their personal behavior as well as the behavior of other human beings as responsible or irresponsible. Most of us also realize that responsible behavior is often not a matter of black or white. Any act or behavior may reflect a degree of responsibility which exists on some measure or continuum of measurement. A responsible or irresponsible act may also be evaluated or perceived in terms of absolutes. For example, many people feel that it is "completely irresponsible" to commit acts of rape or murder under any circumstances.

DEFINITIONS

Most definitions of the word responsible include the concept of liability. For example, *Webster's Ninth New Collegiate Dictionary* (1985) defines responsible as "liable to be called on to answer," "liable to be called on to account as the primary cause, motive, or agent," "being the cause or explanation," "liable to legal review or in case of fault to penalties," "able to answer for one's conduct and obligations: Trustworthy." It is also important to note that Webster's definitions of responsible include "able to answer for oneself between right and wrong," and "politically answerable."

Responsibility is defined as "the quality or state of being responsible; as a: moral, legal, or mental accountability; b: reliability, trustworthiness."

Dictionary-oriented definitions of responsibility consistently emphasize accountability and liability as key components in our understanding of the meaning of this word or concept. Thus, a responsible person or responsible act implies direct moral, legal, or mental liability (accountability) for some event or circumstance. Not only is a responsible person reliable and trustworthy, but he or she is also accountable for the consequences of his or her actions and behaviors. A responsible person is capable of choosing for himself or herself between right and wrong. Therefore, it is implied that a responsible person must somehow understand or know the difference between right and wrong in any given situation in order to make a responsible choice or behave and act responsibly.

MENTAL HEALTH, ADDICTION'S TREATMENT, AND RESPONSIBILITY

Mental health workers have become increasingly concerned about the matter of defining and understanding the concept of "responsible" within the context of their relationships with clients and patients. Unfortunately, behavioral scientists and mental health workers have been unable to consistently agree upon the parameters of responsible (and ethical) therapist and client behavior. For example, is the client ultimately responsible for his or her recovery from alcoholism or some other addictive disease? Is a psychotherapist responsible for his or her client's recovery? What are the "shades" of client and therapist responsibility within the context of a professional psychotherapeutic relationship?

The advent of modern psychiatry, psychology, and behavioral science is marked by clinical and legal confusion associated with the matter of "guilty or not guilty by reason of insanity." This dilemma is ultimately a question of responsibility. Is an insane or mentally deranged person responsible for his or her behavior?

Prichard pointed out in the early 1800s that "a politic, but unscientific objection to the term moral insanity, relates to the disfavor with which the plea of moral insanity as a defense for crime is received by the courts and populace." Early psychiatrists such as Pinel, Prichard, Hughes, and Rush defined moral insanity as "insanity of conduct, feeling or impulse, or all combined, without such appreciable intellectual derangement that it would be recognized as insanity without the display of morbid feeling, impulse or conduct" (Hughes, 1884). These therapists were struggling with the problem of assessing and defining responsible behavior.

Hughes (1884) addressed the matters of physician and patient responsibility at length:

> Questions of consciousness and responsibility constitute pre-established criteria of mental aberration, whereas it is the duty of the physician to determine first the question of mental disease, and after that the degree of consciousness and of responsibility associated with or dependent upon it. There are shades of distinction in the amount of man's presumed responsibility to society, which should be indicated by corresponding shades of punishment when offenses come; but, in all cases, consciousness is presupposed as a condition of responsibleness; so that a disease affecting consciousness renders the agent, so far forth, unfit in kind as well as in degree, to become an object of punishment. Certain phases of irresponsible insanity undoubtedly exist in association with consciousness, while unconscious automatism may be self-induced by certain persons neuropathically endowed, while in a state of responsible insanity. But the degree of insanity should determine the responsibility, not the degree of responsibility the question of insanity" (In Stone, 1896, p. 28).

Early psychiatric exploration of the concept of responsibility soon led to the question of disease. These clinicians were confronted with the problem of separating mental disease and responsibility. Only in very rare cases did "mental disease" and responsibility coexist. Indeed, the early clinicians and behavioral scientists concluded that questions of responsibility belonged to the domain of law, while questions of "disease" belonged to the domain of medicine. It was the duty of the physician to assess and discern the nature of "mental disease" and then enlighten the law as to the relevance of clinical factors associated with the legal question of responsibility.

It is significant that the behavioral science professions and the legal profession continue to grapple with these thorny problems. The apparent insanity of Hinkley resulted in his commitment to a psychiatric hospital rather than incarceration in a state or federal correctional facility following his attempted assassination of President Reagan a few years ago. The "insanity defense" has actually been used by the legal profession for hundreds of years. Yet, psychiatrists and psychologists continue to experience myriad problems in their attempts to differentiate between the irresponsible acts or behaviors of "sane" people and the irresponsible acts of insane persons. These issues are further complicated by the realization that all of us may from time to time experience transient episodes of severe agitation or emotional upheaval which may contribute to (1) situationally determined irresponsible acts and behaviors and (2) an unclear or diminished capacity to differentiate between right and wrong or the responsible-irresponsible dimensions of our behaviors.

The development of psychoanalysis and psychoanalytic theory during the 1900–1950s era generally eroded the concept of personal responsibility as applied to people manifesting neurosis, psychosis, or other forms of mental illness. Generally speaking, it was felt that psychiatric patients were unable to think rationally and behave responsibly as a result of their neuroses and other incapacitating mental aberrations. Freudian psychoanalysis (Mowrer, 1961) asserts that psychoneurosis arises not from moral weakness or failure but from an "excessive and irrational severity or (disease) of the superego or conscience." Psychoanalytic psychotherapy and psychoanalysis attempt to modify patterns of repression and superego development, and thus successful treatment may paradoxically reinforce the development of irresponsible behaviors and acting out! These factors are no doubt related to Eysenck's statement "the success of the Freudian revolution seemed complete. Only one thing went wrong: the patient's did not get any better."

Mowrer (1964) was one of the first contemporary psychotherapists to stress the importance of personal responsibility in healthy behavior. He also believed that irresponsible behavior causes neurosis. Mowrer states that neurosis is "a lie rather than a mistake." Neurotic behavior "begins as a mistake which is then protected and protracted by means of a lie." Psychological symptoms represent the betrayal of the self. These symptoms result from the individual turning against self. They are an outcropping of the truth and an involuntary confession. Symptoms also reflect a distorted but partially healthy attempt upon the part of the distressed person to live and behave more responsibly. Mowrer felt that "therapy" consisted of anything a therapist can do to persuade a neurotic or disturbed person to "voluntarily confess his mistakes, so that conscience does not have to force the truth out of him symptomatically." Thus, the therapist needs to help the patient develop a more open, honest, and responsible style of living.

All modern systems or schools of counseling and psychotherapy stress the importance of both therapist and patient responsibility within the context of the psychotherapy relationship. Perhaps the reality therapists and the cognitive-behavioral therapists are most concerned about the various dimensions of patient and therapist responsibility as they relate to the process and outcome of therapy. The originator of Reality Therapy (Glasser, 1965) emphasizes that people become emotionally disturbed as a result of their irresponsible behaviors and irresponsible life-styles.

Glasser (1965) defines responsibility as

> the ability to fulfill one's needs, and to do so in a way that does not deprive others of the ability to fulfill their needs. . . . A responsible person also does that which gives him a feeling of self-worth and a feeling that he is worthwhile to others. He is motivated to strive and perhaps endure privation to attain self-worth. When a responsible man says he will perform a job for us, he will try to accomplish what was asked, both for us and so that he may gain a measure of self-worth for himself. An irresponsible person may or may not do what he says, depending upon how he feels, the effort he has to make, and what is in it for him. He gains neither our respect nor his own, and in time he will suffer or cause others to suffer.

Doctor Glasser also states "people do not act irresponsibly because they are ill; they are ill because they act irresponsibly." He indicates that people develop various emotional problems because they do not live responsibly in the here and now. The concept of responsibility does not stress the evil in man but rather emphasizes and builds upon man's potential for good. Glasser believes that when people learn to behave more responsibly most of their troubles and problems will clear.

Behaving responsibly is a difficult and complicated lifelong task. Indeed, most people strive to behave and live responsibily. Yet, millions of people have not learned, or have lost the ability, to live and behave responsibly. These people fill our alcohol and drug rehabilitation centers, mental hospitals, prisons, welfare programs, and psychotherapy practices. The teaching and modeling of responsible behavior is the key task of parents, therapists, and mankind. Unfortunately, man lacks an instinct to teach his children responsibility. Responsible living is taught and learned via our intellectual, cognitive, and loving relationships with parents and significant others. Responsible parents teach and model responsible behaviors through their loving, nurturant, and limit-setting relationships with their children. Children usually want to behave responsibly, but they must learn the various skills of responsible living via their relationships with responsible and loving parents and parental models.

The concept of responsibility also encompasses the moral dimensions of behavior. The issues of right and wrong, fairness, honesty, integrity, and truth are important components of responsible behavior and responsible living.

Alcoholics and drug addicts consistently behave irresponsibly. The addictive diseases are rooted in life-styles and behaviors that are highly irresponsible. Addicts and substance abusers become progressively unable to live responsibly. The addiction process fosters and reinforces irresponsible living. Many of these individuals also experienced significant living problems associated with irresponsibility prior to the onset of their addictions.

Psychologists, physicians, alcohol and drug counselors, and other members of the helping professions who work with addicts and substance abusers emphasize that addicted people must learn to become more responsible in order to recover from their addictions. I have indicated (Forrest, 1978)

> a major source of the unhappiness in many alcoholic's lives has been associated with their lack of responsibility. When the addicted person begins to behave in a more responsible fashion he must be reinforced. That the patient has not led a life-style of responsibility should be pointed out early in therapy. One of the therapeutic goals to be initially established is that of increased patient responsibility. The failure to pay bills, work absenteeism, marital infidelities, etc. are all attributes of the patient's irresponsibility and need to be pointed out in the early stages of treatment. The therapist must consistently and unfalteringly expect the patient to change in the direction of increased responsibility. Drinking relapses are interpreted as lapses in responsibility. Once the patient reaches the stage of being able to effectively deal with the responsibility issues pertinent to his own being, he will no longer be dependent upon alcohol as a means of dealing with irresponsibility.

Furthermore, it is virtually impossible for drug addicts and alcoholics to remain "straight" or abstinent in the absence of living and behaving responsibly on a daily basis. This is why it is so important for therapists to "consistently stress the role of generalized patient responsibility throughout all stages of alcoholism psychotherapy" (Forrest, 1984). As Bratter (1985) points out, "addicts become encapsulated by their irresponsible, deceitful, and self-destructive behavior." He goes on to state that effective psychotherapeutic treatment helps addicts assume responsibility for their behavior and thus facilitates the recovery process.

It is equally important for counselors and other helpers who work with substance abusers to maintain responsible life-styles. Irresponsible mental health workers promote and reinforce the irresponsible behaviors of their clients! Optimally effective psychotherapists and change agents model effective and responsible behaviors. Such individuals do not abuse mood-altering chemicals, they pay their bills on time, see clients at the appointed time, and in myriad other ways maintain a responsible style of living. Healthy alcohol and drug counselors (Forrest, 1986) are instruments of healthy prosocial modeling in their relationships with clients.

SUMMARY

All of our lives are governed and shaped by the concept of responsibility. Our irresponsible behaviors create a great deal of heartache, misery, and human suffering. It is clear that alcoholics and severe alcohol abusers are not able to drink responsibly. Alcoholics and addicts hurt themselves and their loved ones as a result of their alcohol-facilitated patterns of irresponsible behavior.

Responsible behavior exists on a continuum, and indeed there are various shades or gradients of responsibility. Social, cultural, interpersonal, situational, and other factors interactively determine the responsible or irresponsible dimensions of an act or behavior.

Several definitions of "responsible" were included in this chapter. In general, responsible may be defined as "causing or being liable for an act." There are significant moral, legal, and mental ramifications associated with all definitions of the word responsible.

Physicians and mental health workers have attempted to define the various parameters of responsibility, sanity and insanity, and the law for two hundred years. Are mentally disturbed or "diseased" individuals legally and morally responsible for their acts and behaviors? Questions such as these are generally difficult to answer, and even the most skilled and experienced of clinicians often disagree on individual cases.

Contemporary counselors and therapists consistently emphasize the importance of client and therapist responsibility within the context of the helping relationship. Clients behave irresponsibly when they "skip" scheduled therapy sessions, fail to pay for professional services, and in other ways violate the agreed-upon dimensions of the treatment relationship. Therapists may also behave irresponsibly in their relationships with various "types" of clients. For example, it is unethical and grossly irresponsible for a therapist to become sexually involved with a client, take drugs or drink with client, or practice under the influence of alcohol.

Glasser (1965) indicates that people develop emotional problems and actually become disturbed as a result of living and behaving irresponsibly. He states "people do not act irresponsibly because they are 'ill'; they are 'ill' because they act irresponsibly." A basic task of the therapist is that of teaching the patient or client more responsible behaviors. Viewed from these perspectives, alcoholics and alcohol abusers develop the disease of alcoholism and all of the various behavioral and emotional problems that accompany the addiction process as a result of their inability to drink responsibly. People who always drink responsibly, in turn, never develop a drinking problem or alcoholism.

Certainly, the ideas and concepts that were discussed in this chapter are subject to debate. It is difficult to know precisely why millions of Americans are problem drinkers and chronic alcoholics. Likewise, it can be very difficult to define "responsible" behavior. Yet, it is very important for you to clearly understand the basic nature and meaning of the concept of responsibility as you read the following chapters in this book. Most of the remaining chapters examine the responsible aspects of drinking within a certain situation or context. You may find it helpful to reread this chapter or parts of this chapter as you reflect upon the nature of *responsible* drinking in each of these different situations.

Chapter 3

PATTERNS OF ALCOHOL CONSUMPTION

DRINKERS AND NON-DRINKERS

Contrary to the beliefs of many, there is a sizable segment of the adult American population that does not drink. In fact, over 20 percent (Forrest, 1986) of adult American's are non-drinkers. These individuals choose not to drink for myriad reasons. This group is comprised of people that formerly consumed alcoholic beverages but for different reasons terminated their use of ethanol, and people that have never imbibed. Some non-drinkers report that they abstain for religious reasons. Several religious denominations do not support the moderate use of alcoholic beverages and some place a very strong emphasis upon the need for total abstinence. Many non-drinkers report that they simply do not enjoy the "taste" or the "effects" of drinking and thus abstain. People in this category also may indicate that they are unable to control their drinking or experience problems as a result of drinking and therefore needed to stop drinking.

Although America is clearly a drinking culture, it is significant that nearly one-fourth of our adults are non-drinkers. It is also important to note that the per capita or percentage of non-drinkers has not changed *radically* over the past several decades. It seems as though there has always been a fairly large segment of our population that has abstained from the use of alcohol. Furthermore, these people remain abstinent for a diversity of reasons.

A basic fact is that non-drinkers are not in any way personally confronted with the matter of coming to grips with the responsible-irresponsible dimensions of their drinking behavior! As non-drinkers, these individuals need not concern themselves with this issue. However, even non-drinkers become the frequent victims of the irresponsible alcohol-facilitated behaviors of drinkers. As such, non-drinkers also need to be cognizant of the various issues associated with responsible and irresponsible drinking.

Most adult Americans are drinkers. As touched upon in earlier chapters, the majority of drinkers are not alcoholics or otherwise irresponsible drinkers. These people seem to be able to consistently control how much alcohol they ingest. They also are able to continue to behave responsibly following drinking. They do not drink compulsively and they are not obsessed with alcohol or the effects of drinking.

Drinkers manifest a diversity of actual drinking styles or patterns of consumption. For example, some drinkers consume primarily wine and beer, while other drinkers may drink only scotch or bourbon. The drinker may imbibe on a daily, weekly, or very infrequent basis. Some drinkers limit their alcohol consumption to New Year's Eve, while others may consume alcoholic beverages at most of the social events they attend.

Broadly speaking, adult drinkers may be classified as (1) social drinkers or moderate drinkers, (2) problem drinkers or alcohol abusers, or (3) alcoholics. Patterns of consumption and styles of drinking may vary considerably within each of these three categories. By definition, drinkers that fall in categories two and three are unable to consistently drink in a responsible manner. Teenagers constitute another category of drinkers.

SOCIAL DRINKERS

Most adult drinkers can accurately be classified as "social drinkers" or moderate drinkers. They drink in moderation and do not experience problems as a result of their drinking. They are normally responsible drinkers. Social drinkers may consume one or two alcoholic beverages per drinking occasion. Such individuals may drink once or twice a week or perhaps far less frequently. A social drinker may consume only three or four alcoholic beverages each year. Yet, social drinking may also describe a pattern of daily consumption that is limited to less than two drinks (2 ounces of ethanol) per day.

Perhaps the key characteristics of social drinkers are their capacities to spontaneously control the use of ethanol and the absence of behavioral, social, legal, and medical problems associated with drinking. Social drinkers are not "worried" about drinking and they do not behave inappropriately after drinking. They are not afraid of alcohol or their behaviors when they do drink. They do not experience significant personality, behavioral, cognitive, or emotional changes after drinking. These individuals do not establish an obsessive-compulsive pattern of alcohol use. Drinking is simply not important to them. They may or may not choose to drink in a given social situation.

It is also significant to note that other people are not concerned or worried about the social drinker's use of alcohol. The spouses and children and close friends of social drinkers are not afraid or anxious about the behaviors of the social drinker following or before drinking. Social drinkers do not experience interpersonal difficulties as a result of their drinking. Their relationships with other people are not centered around drinking and the use of alcohol.

Unfortunately, many problem drinkers and even alcoholics perceive themselves as social drinkers. These individuals are unable to accept the reality of being addicted. They deny being problem drinkers and alcoholics and their denial systems may be reinforced by the irrational belief system that they are "social drinkers." Social drinkers do not feel compelled to drink in order to be social!

It should be noted that heavy drinkers constitute about 15 percent of the drinking populations. Heavy drinkers consume three or four alcoholic beverages or more per drinking occasion and they drink on three occasions or more per week. These people, like social drinkers, may drink to the point of intoxication on an infrequent basis.

In my clinical experience it is logical to expect that at least 30 to 40 percent of heavy drinkers will eventually lose control of their drinking and become problem drinkers or chronic alcoholics. The reader also needs to bear in mind that most alcoholics and alcohol abusers were, in fact, social drinkers before they developed serious drinking problems. I have treated hundreds of alcoholics who were able to drink socially for twenty to thirty years before they began to experience serious drinking problems. In effect, these individuals were responsible drinkers for years, but eventually they became irresponsible drinkers.

PROBLEM DRINKERS

Problem drinkers or alcohol abusers are people that drink excessively, frequently drink to the point of intoxication, and experience family, interpersonal, legal, medical, or economic problems as a direct result of their alcohol consumption. Most of these drinkers do not believe that their drinking is excessive and they usually deny that their major living problems are caused by drinking. Many problem drinkers develop alcohol addiction.

Problem drinkers or alcohol abusers are psychologically dependent upon alcohol. They are *not* physiologically addicted to alcohol. These individuals are usually capable of terminating their drinking behavior for days or even months at a time. Yet, most of their major living problems stem from their abusive and periodically uncontrollable use of alcohol.

The spouse, parents, or children of the problem drinker tend to be worried or concerned about the drinker's use of alcohol. They often realize that the drinker abuses alcohol and yet they are reluctant to openly discuss the drinking issue. Family members may actually reinforce or "enable" the drinker's pathological drinking. Likewise, work associates and colleagues often fall into the trap of drinking with the problem drinker or in other ways enabling his or her drinking behavior. Many alcohol abusers have an uncanny ability to stop drinking and convince others that they are social drinkers.

The simple fact is that problem drinkers experience consistent and significant living problems as a result of their drinking. They can be very difficult to live with. As I have pointed out in my earlier book, *How To Live With A Problem Drinker and Survive,* the prolonged experience of living with an alcohol abuser is an emotional trauma. The spouse or loved ones of the drinker are often in need of therapy and treatment. Adult children of alcoholics and alcohol abusers are psychologically damaged or devastated by the behaviors of the drinker.

There are several different styles of problem drinking and alcohol abuse. Alcohol abusers are always relatively unique human beings. Some may drink in an abusive manner only on the weekends. Others may tend to limit their problem drinking to social functions or perhaps family get-togethers. These are people who abuse alcohol in order to cope with situational or chronic stress. Many people abuse alcohol in order to be more assertive, intimate, or sexual. Problem drinkers may drink abusively in order to initiate or maintain an affair or initiate sexual relationships. In short, there are various factors that cause problem drinking and there are also many different patterns or styles of problem drinking.

I have indicated in several earlier books (see *How to Cope with A Teenage Drinker: New Alternatives and Hope for Parents and Families*) that there are four basic common denominators of a serious drinking problem: (1) drinking compulsively, thus not being able to consistently control such factors as when, where, and how much he or she drinks, (2) drinking for an extended length of time—months or perhaps many years, (3) consistently drinking to the point of intoxication, and (4) experiencing serious interpersonal problems as a result of drinking. Problem drinkers as well as alcoholics manifest these four basic characteristics. We know that approximately one out of every ten adult Americans has a very serious drinking problem.

ALCOHOLICS

Alcoholism has been defined as a progressive and often fatal disease or disorder (Bratter and Forrest, 1985; Mumey, 1986). Alcoholics experience very serious problems in virtually all areas of their lives as a result of their inability to control their drinking. Chronic alcoholics manifest a diversity of internal or psychological, social or interpersonal, economic, legal, spiritual or religious, and medical problems. The alcoholic's total being is adversely effected vis-à-vis his or her relationship with alcohol. Thus, alcoholics are clearly irresponsible drinkers. They seem to have permanently lost their ability to drink responsibly.

Alcohol addiction is a developmental process. It usually takes several months or years for an individual to become alcohol-dependent. However, a minimal alcohol dependence or tissue addiction can occur when a person consumes at least five or six ounces of alcohol daily for approximately one month. Alcoholics are *physically* and *psychologically* addicted to alcohol. An important clinical and diagnostic difference between "alcoholics" and alcohol abusers or "problem drinkers" involves physical dependence. The alcoholic, unlike the alcohol abuser, is physically dependent upon alcohol. Persons who consume a six-pack of beer or four or five martinis a day may think of themselves as "social drinkers" or possibly even "problem drinkers," but they are *physically* and psychologically "hooked" or addicted—they are alcoholics.

Tissue dependence or physiological addiction means that the alcoholic has established a physical tolerance for alcohol and experiences a physical craving and need for alcohol. Alcoholics usually experience physical and psychological withdrawal symptoms when they are unable to continue drinking. Withdrawal symptoms begin to occur after the person has not consumed alcohol for a period of several hours to a few days. These symptoms include irritability, anxiety, agitation, changes in pulse, blood pressure, respiration, and other vital signs. Severe alcohol withdrawal is clinically referred to as delirium tremens or "DTs" and "the shakes." Delirium tremens can be life-threatening. Alcoholics are often shaky and nervous upon rising in the morning, because the withdrawal process actually begins during sleep.

Many alcoholics develop serious medical problems as a result of their drinking. Cirrhosis of the liver, heart disease, kidney damage, neurological impairments, malnutrition, gastrointestinal problems, and various psychiatric/psychological symptoms may be caused by alcohol abuse and alcohol addiction. It is currently estimated that thirteen million Americans have alcoholism.

I have believed for many years that there are several different types or forms of alcoholism. Indeed, every alcoholic is relatively unique with regard to personality makeup, behavioral traits, and even pattern of consumption. Some alcoholics limit their consumption to beer, while others only drink vodka. A basic common characteristic that all alcoholics share is simply the inability to control their drinking. Alcoholics drink in an obsessive-compulsive manner. They continually think about or obsess about alcohol and drinking. They are unable to consistently stop after one or two drinks. One alcoholic beverage may lead to the consumption of twenty alcoholic beverages or perhaps a drunken debauch that lasts for weeks or months.

Alcoholics deny that they are addicted. They usually tell others that they can "quit any time." They tell themselves on hundreds of occasions that they will "quit tomorrow." They blame others for their alcohol dependence. In reality, they are concerned about their drinking behavior, and most of the people around them are concerned about their drinking or clearly realize they are alcoholics. Most alcoholics irrationally believe they can control their drinking, but at the same time they fear the consequences of further drinking. They stop drinking or "go on the wagon" for short periods of time only to "fall off the wagon" or resume drinking on hundreds or thousands of occasions. Alcoholics make themselves and their families and loved ones emotionally upset. The alcoholic family system is severely conflicted and disturbed.

In the absence of effective and long-term treatment the alcoholic is unable to stop drinking, remain abstinent, and recover. Alcoholism is a family disease or illness, and non-addicted family members are also unable to develop and recover without self-help and therapeutic intervention. Alcohol addiction becomes a cancerous emotional plague that is passed on from generation to generation.

Alcoholics seem to be categorically unable to drink responsibly on a consistent basis. Some alcoholics appear to be able to control their drinking and thus give the appearance of drinking responsibly part of the time. Yet, these individuals eventually experience a loss of control over their drinking and become highly irresponsible in many areas of their lives. Alcoholism is a disorder of irresponsibility. Alcoholics are notoriously irresponsible in the areas of paying bills, keeping appointments, following through on commitments, telling the truth, and the overall management of their lives.

TEENAGE DRINKERS

In many respects teenagers constitute a "special" group of drinkers. Regardless of age and age-related state liquor laws, the fact is that most teenagers are drinkers. Like adult drinkers, teenage drinkers manifest various styles or patterns of consumption. By age fourteen about 60 percent of teenagers report they are drinkers. By the time they reach eighteen over 90 percent claim they drink alcoholic beverages. A recent study conducted at the University of Colorado indicated that over 95 percent of college undergraduate students are drinkers.

Is it possible for a teenager to drink responsibly? For example, if a state law requires that people must be at least 18 years of age to consume beer and an 18- or 19-year-old drinks one or two beers at a party, would this be considered responsible or irresponsible? Most would agree that it is irresponsible for a fourteen- or fifteen-year-old to consume several alcoholic beverages. This behavior is a violation of the law and thus irresponsible. How about the fourteen-year-old that consumes only one beer at a dance or social function? These questions and issues will be addressed at length in subsequent chapters. The reader needs to keep these questions in mind as he or she considers the following information and facts about teenage drinking patterns:

(1) Teenagers typically begin to drink between the ages of *twelve and fourteen.*
(2) Twenty-five percent of students in grades seven through twelve drink on a *weekly* basis.
(3) Approximately 4–7 percent of students in grades seven through twelve drink *daily.*
(4) Ten percent of teenagers drink the equivalent of five to twelve alcoholic beverages per drinking occasion per week.
(5) Some 60 percent of teenage Americans get drunk at least once a year.
(6) Over 90 percent of eighteen-year-olds are drinkers.

(7) Several thousand teenagers are killed as a result of drinking and driving each year.
(8) The number of teenagers arrested for drunken driving has more than tripled since 1960.
(9) Nearly 50 percent of adolescent suicides involve intoxication, and
(10) Well over three million teenagers have been treated for alcoholism and alcohol abuse over the past few years.

It is also significant that nearly 20 percent of teenagers report they are experiencing difficulties with their peers as a result of drinking, and nearly 10 percent of teenagers are involved in legal problems because of drinking (Forrest, 1984).

Teenagers also manifest different styles or patterns of consumption. Teenagers tend to be episodic alcohol abusers and experimenters. No doubt many teenagers could be classified as primarily social drinkers. While millions of teenagers experience various drinking problems, most are not alcohol-dependent or addicted. The adolescent years are a time when the vast majority of people experiment with drinking and the effects of alcohol. Experimentation can lead to abuse, addiction, or even death. Alcohol abuse and problem drinking are probably the biggest killers of adolescents and young adults in America.

Parents of teenager drinkers tend to be very concerned about their children's drinking behavior. They are particularly concerned about drinking and driving and alcohol-facilitated accidents. Adolescent drinkers may also be concerned about their drinking as well as the drinking behaviors of friends and peers. Many teenagers are also worried about the drinking patterns of their parents. The combination of alcohol and other mood-altering drugs is a matter of concern for both parents and teenagers.

Teenagers experiment with alcohol and drugs for many different reasons. A variety of factors operate to reinforce teenage patterns of alcohol use, alcohol abuse, and addiction. Peer pressure is not the sole reason that teenagers drink or abuse other chemicals. The drinking styles and behaviors of every teenage drinker are relatively different or unique. Weekend drinking is a common pattern of consumption among teenagers. Drinking at parties, social gatherings, and with peers is common. Most teenagers are moderate consumers of alcohol within these various social contexts. However, many teenagers drink excessively and experience a variety of problems as a result of their drinking behaviors. A small percent of teenage drinkers become problem drinkers and alcoholics very early in their drinking careers. These individuals often have alcoholic parents and they may be genetically programmed to develop alcohol addiction.

It is apparent that teenagers drink alcohol for a diversity of reasons. They also manifest various patterns and styles of consumption. Like their adult counterparts, some are able to drink with control or moderation while others are not. The drinking behavior of some teenagers is clearly irresponsible. Yet, many teenagers seem to be able to drink responsibly. But most adults are realistically frightened by the combination of youth and alcohol. Adolescence is a developmental epoch marked by impulsiveness, conflicts with authority, irresponsibility, individuating and separating from the family, rebellion, heightened sexuality, identity confusion, and emotional immaturity—all behavioral traits of "adult" alcohol abusers and alcoholics. It is little wonder that most parents and adults question the concept of responsible drinking among teenagers!

SOCIOLOGICAL FACTORS ASSOCIATED WITH PATTERNS OF ALCOHOL CONSUMPTION

The consumption of alcoholic beverages constitutes an integral component in the development of most civilizations. Various forms of social interaction incorporate the periodic use of alcohol. Religious activities, business events, festive occasions, medical procedures, and family interactions may incorporate the use of alcohol.

Several years ago it was found that more than twice as many heavy drinkers report never going to church, compared with those attending weekly (Mulford, 1964). Catholics tend to be heavier drinkers than most Protestant groups. Nearly 20 percent of Catholics are heavy drinkers. Methodists, Mormons, and Baptists include low percentages of heavy drinkers. The Jewish also rank very low in percentage of heavy drinkers and alcoholics. Yet, the Jewish religion has one of the highest percentage of drinkers. Ninety percent of Jews are drinkers.

The highest proportion of drinkers are among young men between the ages of twenty-one to thirty-nine in the highest socioeconomic groups. The lowest proportion of drinkers are found within the lowest socioeconomic groups of females over sixty years of age. The incidence of heavy drinking remains relatively constant for all socioeconomic groups. Middle- and upper-class people tend to drink more frequently than lower-class people. However, it is interesting that people in higher socioeconomic groups tend to perceive alcohol consumption as a rather harmless and pleasurable form of social behavior, while people in lower socioeconomic groups perceive drinking and alcohol-related behavior as potentially threatening and dangerous or harmful to the drinker and his family.

Patterns of alcohol consumption are also related to ethnic group membership. For example, Black Americans (Wayne, 1984) experience a high rate of alcoholism, and drinking is widespread among blacks. Alcohol abuse causes many behavioral, social, familial, legal, and medical problems within the black community. The upper as well as lower socioeconomic black groups experience these alcohol-facilitated problems. It is only in the last decade that investigators have begun to systematically investigate patterns of black alcohol consumption.

The Hispanic, Eskimo, and Native American groups have been devastated by problem drinking and alcoholism since their earliest exposure to alcohol. Drinking is pervasive among men and women in these cultures and the incidence of alcohol dependence is very high. Over 50 percent of adult males on some reservations are heavy drinkers or alcoholics. Blood chemistry (Zimberg, 1982) and other physiological factors may partially explain why these groups are so vulnerable to alcoholism and irresponsible drinking. Heavy drinking and drunkenness are expected and socially accepted patterns of consumption with these ethnic groups. Movies and the media have reinforced the stereotype of Native Americans as "drunks" that are obsessed with "firewater." Over 75 percent of all fines, arrests, and legal involvements incurred by Native Americans living on reservations result from drinking. Alcoholism is epidemic among Hispanic, Eskimo, and Native American groups.

Many European groups are notorious for their drinking. Historically, it has been safer to consume alcoholic beverages than water on the European continent. The French and Italians have always been noted for their wine consumption. Men in France drink an average of nearly a quart of wine per day. Women consume about one-fifth of a quart of wine per day. Over one-third of the adult French population drinks more than a quart of wine each day. Many drink more than two quarts per day (Milt, 1969). The lower socioeconomic groups in France consume considerably more wine than the middle and upper socioeconomic levels. The French believe wine is essential to good health, but France has the highest rate of alcoholism in the world (Time, 1974). France also ranks first with reference to per capita level of consumption of absolute alcohol from all alcoholic beverages.

Italians are also wine drinkers. Italian Americans also consume a great deal of wine but appear to have a low incidence of alcoholism and alcohol abuse.

Jewish people tend to drink a great deal but experience a very low incidence of alcoholism. Jews have a long tradition of drinking within the home, at celebrations, within the context of religious ceremonies, and at family gatherings. Jews are often exposed to alcohol and drinking situations, but heavy drinking and alcoholism are not acceptable forms of behavior. As Jewish orthodoxy diminishes, alcohol abuse becomes more prevalent among American Jews.

Irish and Irish Americans are notorious for their inability to drink in moderation. The Irish in America have a long history of high rates of problem drinking and alcoholism. Drinking is frequently associated with arrests for intoxication, drunkenness, assault, and police involvement. Yet, Ireland ranks low nationally with regard to per capita consumption of alcohol. The Irish are reputed drinkers and fighters. There certainly are numerous ethnic jokes that depict Irish Americans as heavy drinkers. By now most of us know what to expect when four Irish Catholic priests get together—a fifth!

Career and occupational status effect patterns of alcohol consumption. Farm owners have had the lowest population of drinkers and heavy drinkers for several decades. Over 80 percent of males comprising the business and professional occupations are drinkers. Nearly 30 percent of businessmen are heavy drinkers. Less than 20 percent of professional males are heavy drinkers. About 40 percent of semiprofessional men are heavy drinkers. Women service workers experience alcohol-related problems and over 15 percent of this group drinks heavily. The more income a man or a woman earns each year, the greater the likelihood he or she will be a drinker.

Successful, wealthy, better-educated, and higher-ranking professional people consistently drink more than poor, uneducated, lower-status individuals. The vast majority of all college graduates report being light or moderate drinkers. Women college graduates are much more likely than other women to be drinkers, but they are much less likely to be heavy drinkers. Those most likely to be heavy drinkers are males who have completed high school and males with some college education but who did not actually graduate from college.

The highest proportion of both drinkers and heavy drinkers are found in the New England, Middle Atlantic, and Pacific regions of the United States. Large cities also have the highest proportion of drinkers, and inner-city residents are most prone to heavy drinking. Rural populations have the smallest percentages of both drinkers and heavy drinkers.

Women have entered the drinker ranks over the past three decades. Some twenty years ago it was believed that one of every nine alcoholics in this country were women. Today, we believe that one of two or one of three alcoholics are women. Working women and professional women are particularly at risk for developing patterns of alcohol abuse and addiction.

In general, Americans of both sexes and Americans of all ages and ethnic backgrounds have frequently reported being drinkers. America is clearly a society of drinkers and a society that is plagued by a diversity of alcohol-related problems. Minority groups have been devastated by alcohol abuse and irresponsible drinking for several decades. Homosexuals, blacks, teenagers, Native Americans, Irish, and other ethnic groups have been perceived as the "outsiders with drinking problems." In reality, these and other ethnic groups constitute America. *We* are the people who are continually confronted with, and live with, or die with the drinking patterns discussed in this chapter.

SUMMARY

Over 20 percent of adult Americans are, in fact, non-drinkers. These individuals choose not to drink for a diversity of reasons. Obviously, the non-drinker is not personally confronted with the matter of responsible drinking. These people are confronted with the problematic and irresponsible drinking of others on a daily basis.

Seven or eight out of ten American adults are drinkers. They can be classified as (1) social drinkers or moderate drinkers, (2) problem drinkers or alcohol abusers, or (3) alcoholics. Teenage drinkers constitute another category of drinkers.

Social drinkers drink in moderation and do not experience problems as a result of their drinking behavior. Moderate drinkers are not "worried" about their drinking, and their families and loved ones are not concerned about drinking. Social drinkers may or may not choose to drink in a given social situation. Social drinkers are able to consistently drink responsibly. It was noted that social drinkers may eventually develop drinking problems.

Problem drinkers experience various psychological, family, social, and legal problems as a result of their drinking. Alcohol abusers or problem drinkers are psychologically dependent upon alcohol, but they are not physically addicted. These individuals are not able to consistently drink responsibly.

Alcoholics are *physically* and *psychologically* addicted to alcohol. Alcoholics experience very serious problems in virtually all areas of their lives as a result of their inability to control their drinking. Alcoholics are also irresponsible drinkers and they have permanently lost the ability to control their drinking. Alcoholics deny they are addicted. Yet, their loved ones are worried about their drinking and realize they are "hooked." Even the alcoholic realizes that he or she is in trouble with alcohol. Alcohol addiction causes irresponsibility and irresponsible patterns of behavior synergistically reinforce further drinking. Irresponsible and uncontrollable drinking are central components in all types of alcoholism.

Teenage drinkers manifest a diversity of drinking styles. However, most teens are experimenters and episodic alcohol abusers. The consumption of alcoholic beverages by underage teenagers is against the law and therefore clearly irresponsible. Yet, over 90 percent of eighteen-year-olds are drinkers, and typically teens begin to consume alcoholic beverages around age thirteen. The key responsibility issues associated with teenage drinking are discussed in subsequent chapters. Youth and alcohol do not mix well. Thousands of teenagers experience a plethora of problems as a result of drinking.

A number of sociological factors are associated with patterns of drinking. Religious affiliation influences style of consumption. Socioeconomic class, sex, education, and age are also associated with patterns of drinking. Ethnic group membership is related to drinking behavior. For example, Native American, Black, Eskimo, young adult male, homosexual, and Irish American ethnic groups tend to experience significant drinking problems. Career and occupational status and even geographical location are related to patterns of drinking. The relationships between these various sociological factors and style or patterns of alcohol consumption were discussed.

It should be apparent to the reader that there are myriad variables that influence a given individual's decision to drink or not drink alcoholic beverages. Furthermore, a diversity of factors determine whether or not an individual drinks responsibly. Many people are able to drink responsibly or socially at one point or time in their lives and not at another. Many alcoholics report that they have never been able to drink responsibly, while others indicate they drank responsibly for many years prior to becoming alcohol-dependent.

An understanding of the patterns of alcohol consumption that are discussed in this chapter will help the reader develop a better appreciation for the complex and often difficult task of assessing the responsible-irresponsible parameters of drinking behavior. Indeed, it may be easy or very difficult to label a particular style or pattern of alcohol use as responsible or irresponsible.

Chapter 4

RESPONSIBLE AND IRRESPONSIBLE DRINKING

DEFINING RESPONSIBLE DRINKING BEHAVIOR

As indicated in Chapter 2, responsible behavior involves being able to satisfy one's basic needs in a rational manner that does not deprive others of the ability to meet their basic needs. Responsible behaviors and responsible living contribute to the development of a positive sense of self-esteem and facilitate a feeling of worth and value to others. Responsible behavior is based upon the concepts of honesty, fairness, truth, and personal integrity. Responsible acts involve moral, legal, and mental accountability. A responsible act also involves doing what is "right" as opposed to behaving in a wrongful or negligent manner.

How do we apply these concepts and principals of responsible behavior to the explicit realm of drinking and the consumption of alcoholic beverages? Is it even possible to evaluate drinking behavior and alcohol use from the perspective of responsible use? No doubt many people believe that there is no such "thing" as responsible drinking or the responsible use of alcohol. Some feel that any use of ethanol is irresponsible, bad, or evil. Most recovering alcoholics have accepted the fact that they cannot drink responsibly, but they wonder if other non-alcoholics are really capable of drinking responsibly. Perhaps most people are confused about the idea of responsible drinking. They simply are not sure what "responsible drinking" means.

In fact, there are no simple or easy answers to these questions. Sometimes it may be difficult to define responsible drinking. This is also a confusing issue. Some people drink responsibly most or part of the time but not all the time. As discussed in Chapter 3, responsible drinking may be viewed or defined differently according to one's ethnic, educational, or social background.

In spite of these obstacles and barriers to defining responsible drinking behavior, I believe that it is possible to develop operational and pragmatic guidelines for responsible as well as irresponsible drinking.

The broad parameters of responsible and irresponsible drinking that were outlined in Chapter 3 will be more precisely delineated in this chapter.

Responsible drinking behavior is consuming alcohol in a manner that is no way injurious to the psychological, interpersonal, physical, moral, legal, or spiritual well-being of the drinker, society, or other people. Responsible drinkers are able to limit the frequency and level or amount of alcohol they consume. They do not in any way crave alcohol or the effects of drinking, and they do not experience significant personality and behavioral changes after imbibing. Alcohol ingestion does not precipitate internal feelings of depression, guilt, anxiety, fear, or anger in the responsible drinker. These individuals do not experience behavioral, health, legal, social, or familial problems as a result of their drinking. Drinking alcohol is basically not an important matter to these individuals. They do not *need* to drink and they find it easy to choose not to drink. They are not concerned about their drinking, nor are their families, loved ones, work associates, or significant others. Responsible drinkers are in no way controlled or obsessed with alcohol. These drinkers are also first and foremost legally old enough to consume alcoholic beverages.

I have observed many different patterns of responsible drinking. Some of these drinkers consume only three or four alcoholic drinks each year. They may drink a glass of champagne or two on New Year's Eve or perhaps on their birthdays. Others may have one drink nightly or perhaps one to three drinks on a monthly or weekly basis. They maintain their personal style of drinking for months, years, or a lifetime. They do not progressively consume more alcoholic beverages over time or experience a progressive loss of control over their drinking behavior. These drinkers are able to maintain a *consistently* responsible pattern of alcohol use. Responsible drinkers do not find it necessary to drink to the point of intoxication. They may enjoy the taste or mild effects of an alcoholic beverage with friends or in combination with a meal or social event.

Alcohol ingestion does not impair the responsible drinker's capabilities to meet his or her various needs in an appropriate manner and does not interfere with the abilities of others to fulfill their basic needs. Drinking does not undermine the responsible drinker's sense of self-worth and does not depreciate his or her value to others. The drinker does not behave dishonestly or become immoral, mentally impaired, or a liar as a result of drinking. Responsible drinkers do not undermine their sense of personal pride, integrity, and dignity as a result of drinking.

Drinking does not erode the responsible drinker's spiritual and religious beliefs, values, behaviors, or relationships with God or the church.

These basic guidelines for responsible drinking and characteristics of responsible drinkers will be applied to several practical situations that all of us are periodically confronted with in the following chapters of this book. For the most part, these practical or everyday situations involve the responsible drinking issue within such contexts as parents and children, parties and social gatherings, office parties and festive occasions, personal health, and driving.

DEFINING IRRESPONSIBLE DRINKING BEHAVIOR

Any use of alcohol that is detrimental to the psychological, physical, interpersonal, moral, legal, or spiritual well-being of the drinker, society, or other people is irresponsible. In a simplistic sense, irresponsible drinking is the converse of responsible drinking.

As noted in Chapter 3, problem drinkers or alcohol abusers and alcoholics are *ipso facto* irresponsible drinkers. Irresponsible drinkers harm themselves, their families and loved ones, and society via their drinking behaviors. For example, alcoholics literally destroy themselves through the medium of alcohol and their pathologic relationships with ethanol. Adult children of alcoholics (Black, 1981) represent the emotional carnage of alcoholism and the experience of being parented by an alcoholic. Alcohol abusers hurt themselves in myriad ways as a result of their uses of ethanol.

Alcoholism is literally a disease or disorder of the whole person. Addiction is a disease that destroys the physical, psychological, moral, social, and spiritual well-being of its victims. Alcoholism and alcohol abuse result in acting-out and irresponsible behaviors. Indeed, alcohol intoxication may facilitate transient irresponsible acts in social drinkers as well as alcohol abusers. In many respects, it matters very little whether or not an alcoholic behaved responsibly or irresponsibly before the onset of his or her pathological drinking. The fact is that alcohol addiction or abuse causes irresponsible behavior. Intoxication results in neurologic, biophysiological, and organismic changes that affect judgment, reasoning, emotional control, and motor behavior. The effects of alcohol intoxication in all of the cognitive or intellectual aspects of human behavior can cause irresponsible thinking, emoting, and behaving.

Irresponsible drinkers are often unable to consistently limit or control the amount of alcohol they consume. Many irresponsible drinkers are preoccupied about alcohol and drinking. They are unable to control how much they drink once the drinking process begins. Perhaps most importantly, irresponsible drinkers behave irresponsibly after they consume one or several alcoholic beverages. These people experience a global loss of control following drinking. Irresponsible drinkers may become angry, depressive, seductive, or clearly sociopathic following drinking. Irresponsible drinkers display significant personality and behavioral changes when they drink.

Drinking does impair the irresponsible drinker's ability to meet his or her needs in an appropriate manner. Alcohol usè also impairs the irresponsible drinker's capacity to meet the needs of the loved ones and significant others in his or her life. The drinking behaviors of irresponsible drinkers interfere with the abilities of their loved ones to meet their own basic needs. For example, the wives and children of irresponsible drinkers often become so depressed, guilty, angry, and anxious that they are unable to manage their lives in a healthy and rational manner. Life with a problem drinker can be hell (Forrest, 1986)!

Drinking eventually destroys the irresponsible drinker's sense of self-worth. Intoxication, drinking, and the alcohol-facilitated irresponsible behaviors of the drinker clearly depreciate and erode his or her value to significant others. Irresponsible drinkers tend to be manipulative, conning, dishonest, and without a healthy sense of personal pride or dignity. These people often distort reality, lie, and blame others for their irresponsible drinking. The irresponsible drinker is eventually unable to like or love himself or others. A narcissistic obsession with self and alcohol pervades the drinker's relationships with self, others, and the world.

Irresponsible drinking may completely errode the drinker's moral, ethical, and spiritual values and beliefs. Alcoholics are invariably conflicted in their relationships with God, the church, and spirituality. They are plagued with feelings of guilt about their drinking, irresponsible behaviors, and needs for some form of spiritual or religious meaning in life. These individuals feel trapped and turn to further drinking and intoxication as solutions for their myriad living problems.

Many are unable to give up their attempts to control their drinking and die in the process. These unfortunates seem to be completely unable to accept the reality that they cannot drink responsibly. Most irresponsible drinkers put a great deal of time, emotional effort, and money into their efforts to convince self and others that they can drink responsibly.

They want to be social drinkers and they delude themselves with this illusion on hundreds or thousands of occasions. In spite of the realities of hangovers, arrests, family problems and divorces, health complications, sexual problems, and career or educational shortcomings, they struggle to be responsible drinkers.

It is usually easy to identify and comprehend the irresponsible dimensions of the drinking behaviors of alcoholics and alcohol abusers. It can be more confusing and difficult to identify the irresponsible drinking behaviors of social drinkers. Most social or moderate drinkers can and, in fact, actually do drink irresponsibly from time to time. The social drinker who consumes five or six drinks once every several years instead of his or her "usual" of one or two drinks may be drinking irresponsibly. A hangover or general malaise resulting from "one or two" too many can be considered irresponsible drinking. If a social drinker does experience the physical symptoms of a hangover once every year or once every 10 years, then it is reasonable to assume that this individual is a very infrequent irresponsible drinker.

Perhaps a more common example of irresponsible drinking upon the part of social drinkers involves drinking and driving. The drinker who attends a cocktail party or office party and then drives home after consuming three or four alcoholic drinks in a period of one or two hours is an irresponsible drinker. In fact, driving a vehicle after consuming any amount of alcohol may constitute an irresponsible act. While social drinkers may only drink and drive once a year or once every three or four years, such behavior nonetheless involves irresponsible drinking. Many, if not most, moderate or social drinkers may infrequently drink irresponsibly. All drinkers can even be considered potential alcohol abusers or alcoholics, and certainly every drinker is a potential irresponsible drinker.

A great deal of confusion over the matter of responsible vs. irresponsible drinking is associated with the generally non-dichotomous nature of drinking behavior. Drinking behavior can be viewed from a continuum-oriented perspective, and it may be very difficult to accurately know when a given individual's drinking behavior is or becomes absolutely irresponsible or responsible. As suggested in earlier chapters, there are "shades" of irresponsibility and responsibility associated with all acts and behaviors.

In this regard, even the drinking behaviors and consumption styles of many chronic alcoholics can be superficially baffling and give the inconsistent appearance of responsible drinking. A great many alcoholics are notorious for their ability to remain totally abstinent or control their drinking behaviors for weeks or perhaps months at a time. However, virtually all drinking or non-recovering alcoholics return to a pattern of addictive and irresponsible drinking. They may deceive themselves and significant others into believing that they are no longer alcoholic drinkers during their intervals of abstinence. Yet, the uncontrollable and irresponsible nature of their addictive disease consistently becomes manifest shortly after they begin to imbibe. Alcoholics and severe alcohol abusers are consistently unable to drink responsibly once they initiate the actual drinking process. They may appear to be drinking responsibly for a few hours, days, or weeks, but eventually they are grossly out of control and re-experience the same destructive pattern of addictive behaviors, thoughts, emotions, and alcohol-facilitated irresponsible styles of living.

SUMMARY

All forms of responsible behavior involve being honest, fair, truthful, moral, and satisfying one's basic needs in a rational manner that does not in any way injure or limit the need-satisfying behaviors of others.

What is responsible drinking? While some may believe that any use or ingestion of ethanol is irresponsible, in this chapter responsible drinking behavior is defined as consuming alcohol in a manner that is in no way injurious to the psychological, interpersonal, physical, moral, or spiritual well-being of the drinker, society, or other people. The various parameters of responsible drinking are elucidated in this chapter. Responsible drinkers consume small amounts of alcohol; they are not obsessed with alcohol and/or the effects of drinking; they do not drink compulsively, and they do not experience significant personality and behavioral changes following drinking. They may enjoy the taste of an alcoholic beverage or they enjoy "a drink" with a meal or in the context of a special social event. These drinkers maintain a *consistent* pattern of responsible consumption.

It is significant that drinking alcohol is not an important or obsessive matter for the responsible drinker or his or her family and loved ones. They are simply not concerned or worried about drinking. The use of alcohol does not in any way interfere with the responsible drinker's life. Drinking does not undermine the responsible drinker's sense of self-worth and does not depreciate his or her value to others.

Responsible drinkers are able to control their drinking, and drinking is an integrated component of their life-style. They drink alcoholic beverages and enjoy drinking for various reasons, but they are able to imbibe without behaving irresponsibly in any area of daily living.

Irresponsible drinking is defined as use of alcohol that is detrimental to the psychological, physical, interpersonal, moral, or spiritual well-being of the drinker, society, or other people. Alcoholics and problem drinkers or alcohol abusers are unable to drink responsibly. Irresponsible drinkers harm themselves, their loved ones, and society as a result of this drinking.

The various irresponsible dimensions of alcoholic drinking and alcohol abuse were discussed in this chapter. Addiction is a disease of the total person. Thus, these drinkers are categorically irresponsible drinkers. Irresponsible drinkers are preoccupied about alcohol and drinking. They drink compulsively and thus cannot control their use of alcohol. They frequently drink to the point of intoxication and behave irresponsibly in many areas of their lives. These drinkers manifest various pathologic behavioral and personality changes after drinking. They drink for effect rather than enjoyment, taste, or because of other healthy reasons. Addicts experience a craving for alcohol and intoxication and they use any reason or rationalization in the service of their addiction, be it a promotion, job loss, sunny day, or marital problems.

Irresponsible drinkers frequently attempt to convince themselves and others that they can control their drinking, that they are responsible drinkers! This can be a confusing issue. In fact, many responsible drinkers eventually become alcoholics and irresponsible drinkers. Alcoholics and alcohol abusers may appear to be responsible drinkers on a short-term basis. However, these drinkers are unable to maintain a consistently responsible pattern of consumption. Social drinkers or moderate drinkers may periodically drink irresponsibly. Indeed, it may be very difficult to accurately know when a given individual's drinking behavior is or becomes absolutely irresponsible or responsible. There are shades of responsibility and irresponsibility associated with all types or patterns of alcohol use.

A final word about the controversial issue of alcoholics and severe alcohol abusers reversing their destructive and irresponsible patterns of alcohol consumption is in order. It is possible or probable that alcoholics can learn to drink responsibly? This controversial issue has never been satisfactorily resolved within the alcoholism treatment field. Controlled drinking has remained a matter of controversy for over forty years in the alcoholism treatment field. However, in seventeen years of clinical practice with alcoholics and alcohol abusers I have never worked with or observed a primary alcoholic who has been able to maintain a long-term pattern of controlled and responsible ethanol consumption—*not one!* Yet, many episodic alcohol abusers do develop the capacity to drink responsibly and in moderation (Zimberg, 1982). Such may be the case with or without professional alcoholism or alcohol abuse treatment.

Roughly 75 percent of college students are periodic alcohol abusers and problem drinkers. However, less than 15 percent of these individuals progress into alcoholism or remain alcohol abusers after they enter their late twenties. These individuals seem to spontaneously give up their patterns of episodic irresponsible drinking. Unfortunately and sometimes tragically, it is impossible to predict which individuals will mature into responsible patterns of consumption. These emotional and confusing realities have long been associated with our professional reluctance to address the issue of responsible vs. irresponsible alcohol use.

The remaining chapters in this book will examine the responsible and irresponsible aspects of drinking in several contexts that are of practical importance to all of us—parents, adolescents, drivers, and employers and workers.

Chapter 5

PARENTAL DRINKING BEHAVIORS AND ATTITUDES TOWARD ALCOHOL USE: EFFECTS ON CHILDREN

PARENTS WHO DRINK

Most parents are drinkers. Drinking parents manifest various styles of drinking. One spouse may be a non-drinker while the other is a moderate drinker or perhaps a heavy drinker. Both spouses may be non-drinkers or both might be alcoholics. In all of these situations, parents differ with regard to drinking or not drinking, style of consumption, and beliefs and attitudes about alcohol use. Marital partners may or may not share similar styles of consumption. Likewise, they may or may not share similar attitudes and beliefs about drinking and alcohol use.

Parental patterns of consumption, or non-drinking, as well as beliefs and attitudes about drinking and the use of alcohol affect children in a multiplicity of ways. What are the specific effects of parental drinking upon children? How do the attitudes of parents toward alcohol and drinking impact upon the beliefs and attitudes of their children toward drinking or life in general? Do children eventually learn to drink responsibly, abusively, or alcoholically as a result of their parent's drinking behaviors? It is very difficult to answer questions such as these in a definitive manner. Yet, we are beginning to conduct clinical and research studies which suggest possible solutions and clues to the ultimate answers to questions such as these.

It is clear that our parents and families are our earliest teachers. Many of our earliest, most basic, and profound learning experiences occur within the context of our early life parental and family relationships. Parents or surrogate parents teach us basic eating habits, how to dress ourselves, tie our shoes, and the other rudimentary living and survival skills. They also teach us to like ourselves or dislike ourselves and profoundly influence our sense of basic self-worth. Our basic beliefs, attitudes, values, perceptions, behaviors, and thinking and feeling styles are influenced by our parents vis-à-vis the total experience of some eighteen or more years of family living.

Parents and significant others teach us all these things through a wide variety of teaching devices. They verbally tell us how to evaluate ourselves, how to understand our world and our experiences, and they tell us what to believe and how to think. Parents profoundly shape the development of our verbal and social communicative skills. They also teach us through the medium of their behaviors. This is called imitative learning or modeling. As young children, adolescents, and even adults we watch and observe the behaviors of our parents and significant others. We learn many effective as well as ineffective patterns of behavior by watching and imitating our parents.

Our parents also teach us a great deal about alcohol and drinking. We vicariously observe that our parents consume alcoholic beverages, don't drink, drink in a certain manner, or that they believe certain things about drinking. We do this by watching them and listening to their communications about alcohol use. In fact, it has been reported (Health Communications, 1978) that 6 out of 10 seventh graders who indicate that they are drinkers had their initial drinking experience with their parents on a special occasion. Thus, parents frequently introduce their children to drinking and alcohol use. However, parents really begin to communicate their personal beliefs and attitudes about drinking to their children when they are very young. Young children observe the drinking behaviors and attend to the alcohol-related verbal and non-verbal communications of their drinking parents from the time of infancy until their interactions with their parents end.

Drinking parents communicate to their children a diversity of positive or negative messages about alcohol use. When parents introduce their children to alcohol by drinking with them, they are clearly teaching and telling them that it is okay to drink. They also teach their children how to "mix" drinks, that it is acceptable to drink wine but not beer, that one or two alcoholic drinks are okay but several drinks are not, or that intoxication and violence result from drinking. Whenever children are around drinking parents they are continuously learning about alcohol, the effects of alcohol, and drinking. Again, these alcohol-oriented, parental-facilitated learning experiences may be positive or negative.

Children that grow up in alcoholic homes also learn a great deal about alcohol and drinking from their alcoholic parent or parents. These alcohol-oriented and parental-facilitated learning experiences are traumatic and pathologic. The alcoholic parent eventually teaches his or her children how to drink, how to drink and behave alcoholically, and thus programs them for an addictive life-style. At least 30 to 40 percent of the children of alcoholics eventually become alcoholics or drug-dependent. Aside from the causative matters of genetics and brain chemistry in alcoholics, these children continually learn from their alcoholic parent various patterns of behavior, thinking, communicating, relating, and feeling that are central to the development of alcoholism and alcohol abuse. It is not surprising that so many of the children of alcoholics eventually become alcoholics!

It should also be noted that about 15 percent of children of alcoholics do not become adult drinkers. I recently saw the seventeen-year-old son of a drinking alcoholic in therapy. He told me four times in our initial session "I never want to be like my father—he's the last person I would ever want to turn out like." The boy's father was a seemingly successful and well-educated superintendent of a large school system. His father consumed fifteen to twenty alcoholic beverages each evening! His son did not drink, did not use other drugs, and he verbalized a very angry attitude toward all alcohol use. It was very easy to understand this patient's feelings and attitudes toward drinking.

Adult children of alcoholics who are non-drinkers or moderate drinkers consistently exhibit a pattern (Black, 1981) of personality and behavior flaws. Although they are not alcohol-dependent, they have learned a number of maladaptive alcoholic behaviors and developed certain personality problems as a result of the experience of being parented by an alcoholic. ACA's tend to have problems expressing their feelings. They are often depressive, insecure, manipulative, anxious, and have low self-worth. It should also be noted that roughly 25 to 35 percent of ACA's are infrequent or moderate drinkers.

It has been reported by the NIAAA that over 80 percent of families in which both parents drink produce children who drink. Indeed, several studies have found that the sons and daughters of drinking parents usually drink. Parental drinking style also affects the development of drinking patterns in children. Aside from the causal relationship between parental alcoholism and offspring alcoholism, we do not know the *precise* relationships between moderate or social drinking in parents and drinking styles of offspring. The children of moderate and non-drinking parents may also develop alcoholism and various patterns of alcohol abuse. However, the vast majority of children that have parents who are moderate drinkers do not become alcoholics and problem drinkers.

It was reported several years ago (Bales, 1946; Snyder, 1958) that virtually all American Jews have early and frequent experiences with drinking alcoholic beverages, but few evidence problems with drinking. Jewish children are introduced to drinking by their parents and they begin to drink at a very early age. Yet, relatively few Jews become alcoholics or severe alcohol abusers. Why is this so? A number of familial and sociocultural factors have been linked to the general pattern of Jewish alcohol consumption. Drinking with meals and within the family context, the idea of "good things in moderation" and "excess is shameful," and strong ingroup-outgroup identification with moderate drinking are sociocultural defererents to alcohol abuse among Jews (Heath, 1983). However, it should also be noted that Jews do not have the relative immunity from alcoholism and drinking problems that they had twenty or thirty years ago. As Jews have become integrated into the business, professional, and social life of gentile society they seem to have developed more drinking and alcohol-related problems.

It is apparent that drinking parents do influence or shape the manner in which their children consume alcohol. Unfortunately, it is very difficult to know or predict *precisely* how individual cases of parental drinking impact upon the drinking behaviors of a specific child or children. There are several very general but consistent relationships between parental style of alcohol use and offspring drinking behaviors: (1) drinking parents reinforce alcohol use among their children, (2) an alcoholic parent, alcoholic parents, or parents that are severe alcohol abusers have children that are very susceptible to developing alcoholism and drinking problems, and (3) parents that drink very little or in moderation, and parents that do not have drinking problems, consistently have children that are not alcoholics or severe alcohol abusers.

There are caveats and exceptions to these general findings. Nonetheless, research evidence such as that reported by Orford (1985), indicating "children whose fathers were light drinkers and whose parents both had relatively disapproving attitudes towards their drinking, had a 2.5-to-1 chance of being light drinkers themselves, whereas those with heavy drinking fathers and parents who approved of their drinking had more than a 3 to 1 chance of being relatively heavy drinkers themselves" (p. 121) clearly demonstrates that parents and parental models can directly affect (1) their children's decision to drink alcohol and (2) the pattern of consumption their children develop.

NON-DRINKING PARENTS

It was pointed out earlier in this chapter that most parents are, in fact, drinkers and that drinking parents teach their children a diversity of behaviors, attitudes, and beliefs about alcohol and drinking vis-à-vis their personal relationships with alcohol. Likewise, non-drinking parents may teach their children a great deal about alcohol use and drinking through their personal *non-use* of alcoholic beverages.

Parental messages about alcohol use are probably most potent and consistent when both parents either drink or abstain. Thus, when both parents are non-drinkers their children are exposed to fewer ambivalent attitudes, beliefs, feelings, and behaviors that are associated with alcohol use and drinking.

It is important to simply realize that most parents in our culture do not abstain from alcohol use. Families that include parents who are non-drinkers communicate to their children that it is "ok" or socially appropriate to abstain from drinking and alcohol use. This is a very basic but important parental message. The verbal, behavioral, emotional, and relationship dimensions of this form of parental message gives children permission to: (1) say "no" to alcohol use—to choose not to drink, (2) deviate from an accepted sociocultural norm and not feel threatened or stigmatized as a result of this choice, and (3) consolidate a healthy non-drinking identity.

The NIAAA (1978) has reported that 72 percent of parents who are non-drinkers produce children who do not drink. This finding suggests that non-drinking parents do shape and influence their children's beliefs, attitudes, and behaviors relative to drinking and alcohol use. More specifically, parental non-drinking fosters the development of abstinence and the choice not to drink in children. This trend is consistent throughout adolescence and adulthood, although the children of non-drinking parents become progressively more apt to use alcohol with increasing age.

Although it is clear that non-drinking parents teach and model non-drinking behaviors to their children, they may do this in a variety of ways. First of all, non-drinking parents are obviously behavioral models who reinforce abstinence. They may or may not verbally teach their children to abstain and the verbal set or style of teaching children to be non-drinkers may vary considerably between parents or among non-drinking sets of parents. Abstinent parents may employ a diversity of attitudes and beliefs in their conscious or unconscious efforts to teach their children to abstain. While these parental teaching efforts seem to be generally successful in providing abstinence in children, they may result in several different beliefs or reasons for non-drinking upon the part of children. For example, some non-drinking parents may repeatedly tell their children that any use of alcohol will result in alcoholism. Other abstinent parents may teach their children that alcohol use is "forbidden" in their family or that members of their religion simply do not imbibe. In short, parents may tell their children not to drink for many reasons. They may base their non-drinking verbal messages on their religious affiliation, family history of alcohol abuse, morality, or fear. No doubt, they communicate their *personal* beliefs and reasons for abstaining to their children and hope that these will be deterrents to drinking for their children.

Non-drinking parents communicate many positive, rational, responsible messages to their children by their non-drinking behaviors. These parents teach their children that it is not necessary to drink in order to relax, socialize, or escape the many stresses and problems of daily living. They teach their children that intimacy, love, and even sexual relatedness are not associated with drinking and alcohol use. It is extremely important for adolescents in particular to learn the various social skills that are needed to develop friendships, love relationships, and healthy modes of human interaction. Adolescents need to develop these various social skills in the absence of drinking and drug use. Abstinent parents can be healthy role models who communicate to their children that alcohol is not an important ingredient in social interactions. These parents teach their sons and daughters that they do not need to drink in order to be socially assertive, communicative, ask for dates, or deal with the other interpersonal and intrapersonal struggles of adolescence.

In some situations it is possible that non-drinking parents actually contribute to the development of drinking problems in their children. When parents consistently tell their children that any use of alcohol is wrong or evil and that drinking will lead to alcoholism or moral depravity, they may actually foster drinking. Rebellious adolescents and adolescents who manifest acting-out problems are especially prone to "testing" parental injunctions against drinking. These adolescents assume that drinking must be fun and exciting if their parents are so convinced that it is "bad," immoral, or in other ways unacceptable to imbibe. In effect, they choose to drink as a means of rebelling against their parents. These children may be prone to developing serious drinking problems. Parental disapproval of drinking can foster feelings of guilt, ambivalence, and anger in the child who drinks against the wishes of his or her parents. These children use alcohol for all the wrong reasons. They drink with destructive emotions, and they have not been exposed to responsible drinking parental role models.

Research (Heath, 1983) suggests that when individuals break cultural, religious, or strong familial rules and mores against drinking they are more susceptible to developing drinking problems. For example, members of the Mormon religion are advocates of total abstinence. Mormon's who break the taboo or religious dictate against alcohol use run the increased risk of becoming alcohol abusers. Yet, it is important to recognize that strong cultural, religious, and familial taboos or rules against drinking are generally effective deterrents to drinking.

There are also many parental dyads in which one spouse is a drinker while the other is abstinent. In family situations where a drinking parent is not an alcohol abuser and there are no marital or family conflicts associated with the drinker's use of alcohol it is likely that children will not develop drinking problems or pathologic attitudes and beliefs about alcohol use. However, there are also thousands of families that experience severe marital and familial dissonance over the drinking patterns of a spouse/parent. One parent may be alcoholic or a severe alcohol abuser, while the other parent is abstinent or perhaps a moderate drinker. The drinking/non-drinking oriented conflicts that occur in these families clearly impact upon the alcohol use, beliefs, and attitudes of children. Conflicts and confusion over alcohol use may even exist in situations where the drinking parent is clearly not an alcoholic or alcohol abuser if the non-drinking spouse perceives any use of alcohol as somehow unacceptable or deviant. Children in these situations are the recipients of "mixed messages" about drinking and alcohol use. They can develop many confused and ambivalent beliefs and feelings about drinking, and these children may be at risk for developing drinking problems.

Some twenty to thirty million (Black, 1981) Americans are the adult children of alcoholics. Many of the alcoholic parents of these children of alcoholics have stopped drinking when they were children or adolescents. Yet, these ACA's have been significantly and negatively affected by the drinking behaviors of their addicted parent or parents. Recovering alcoholics are non-drinking parents. Understandably, these parents tend to fear that their children will eventually develop alcoholism or a serious chemical dependency problem. Even in families that include a non-drinking and recovering alcoholic parent it is reasonable to expect that 20 to 30 percent of the children will develop a serious drinking problem. Recovering parents and ACA's need to be aware of these facts. They also need to consistently and rationally attempt to educate their children about alcohol and alcohol use. Unfortunately, adult ACA's as well as recovering alcoholics may sometimes unwittingly reinforce the development of a drinking disorder in their children via (1) the perception and belief that any use of alcohol will result in alcoholism, (2) ambivalence about setting limits on the drinking behaviors of their children, (3) failure to openly and honestly share with children their personal and familial history of alcoholism, and (4) the use of "iron-fisted" disciplinary tactics that are intended to stop (or control) their children's use of alcohol.

It is apparent that non-drinking parents can play various roles in the process of shaping and affecting their children's beliefs, perceptions, and attitudes about alcohol. They influence their children's decisions to drink or abstain and they also affect children's style of consumption. These parental influences can reinforce patterns of alcohol abuse, addiction, abstinence, or responsible drinking. In short, the issues of parental use of alcohol and parental attitudes about drinking can affect children in a "for better or for worse" manner. Even the genes of the non-drinking and recovering alcoholic parent may influence, or determine, the drinking behaviors of a son or daughter.

SUMMARY

The drinking patterns or abstinence, and beliefs, attitudes, and perceptions of parents influence their children's decisions and beliefs about alcohol use. Parents and significant others educate children about drinking and alcohol use very early in life and throughout the course of their parenting relationships. Parents use various alcohol-oriented teaching techniques in their interactions with their children. They may verbally tell their children that alcohol use in moderation is acceptable, that drinking is taboo, or that heavy drinking is essential to success in the business world. They behaviorally model and teach various beliefs, behaviors, and attitudes about alcohol use.

Drinking parents teach their children a plethora of things about alcohol use. The initial drinking experiences of most children actually take place with their parents. Drinking parents have children who consistently become drinkers. Indeed, there are several general and consistent relationships between parental style of alcohol use and offspring drinking behaviors: (1) drinking parents reinforce alcohol use among their children, (2) an alcoholic parent or parents with severe drinking problems have children that are at risk for developing alcoholism or a drinking disorder, and (3) parents who drink in moderation and do not have drinking problems consistently have children that are not alcoholics or problem drinkers. Again, it is clear that drinking parents do influence their children in the specific areas of choosing to drink or abstain and style of consumption.

It also needs to be emphasized that there are exceptions to these general relationships between parental drinking and offspring drinking. The children of alcoholics are sometimes non-drinkers or social drinkers. The children of moderate drinkers and abstainers sometimes do develop alcohol addiction or a serious drinking problem. Perhaps it is well to bear in mind that we are all biologically addictive, and thus all human beings are potential alcohol abusers and alcoholics!

Non-drinking parents are a minority group in America. However, abstinent parents also teach their children a diversity of beliefs, attitudes, and behaviors that are associated with alcohol and alcohol use. They may globally communicate to their children that drinking is unacceptable or "bad." They may openly and rationally share the reasons for their personal decision not to imbibe with their children. Some non-drinking parents feel compelled not to drink as a result of their religious beliefs or affiliations and they may share these realities with their children.

It is important to note that non-drinking parents do have children that are more frequently non-drinkers. Thus, these parents seem to foster in their children the decision not to use alcohol. The NIAAA has found that over 70 percent of parents who are non-drinkers have children who are also non-drinkers.

Abstinent parents can teach their children many rational and healthy messages via their non-use of alcohol. These parents teach and demonstrate to their children that alcohol is not needed for purposes of relaxation, socialization, stress management, or having fun.

It was also noted that non-drinking parents may possibly contribute to the development of drinking problems in their children. Some adolescents may rebell against parental dictates or messages associated with abstinence and as a result of having not had responsible drinking parental models, perhaps drinking with guilt and ambivalence, and using alcohol as a tool for adolescent rebellion, they experience drinking problems.

Finally, there are many parental dyads that include both a drinking and non-drinking parent or parents with different combinations of drinking styles and attitudes and beliefs about alcohol use. Children who grow up in families that include parents with highly divergent and conflicted patterns of alcohol consumption as well as radically differing beliefs and attitudes toward alcohol use are prone to develop drinking problems. Individual, parental and familial, and cultural ambivalence about drinking and alcohol use contributes to the development of drinking problems and high rates of alcoholism. In general, Americans are very ambivalent about drinking and alcohol use—perhaps we are as ambivalent about our drinking as we are about sex and our sexuality!

Finally, the impact of parental alcoholism on children was discussed. Recovering parents and adult children of alcoholics need to be aware of the many realities that can foster the development of drinking problems in their children. They also need to continually educate their children about these realities in a manner which does not include the pitfalls which reinforce alcohol abuse in ACA's and the children of recovering alcoholics. The pitfalls which frequently reinforce the development of drinking problems in ACA's and the children of recovering alcoholics are also outlined in this chapter.

Chapter 6

GUIDELINES FOR RESPONSIBLE PARENTAL DRINKING

PARENTS WHO DRINK RESPONSIBLY

As discussed in Chapter 5, most parents do drink alcoholic beverages. Most parents are also responsible drinkers—at least, most of the time! This is an important issue, as responsible drinkers, by definition, are people who are able to *consistently* drink in a responsible manner.

Parents who drink responsibly share several common behavioral characteristics that pertain to their use of ethanol. They also tend to share certain beliefs and attitudes about alcohol and drinking. These parents drink in moderation. They are generally infrequent users of alcohol. They rarely, if ever, drink to the point of intoxication. They are open about their drinking and they are very much aware of the dimensions of both responsible alcohol use and irresponsible alcohol use. They communicate honestly and openly with their children about drinking and alcohol use, and they actively teach their children about responsible alcohol use.

The behaviors, attitudes, and communications of parents who drink responsibly are very consistent. For example, these parents do not drink one glass of wine with their meal on some occasions and then consume ten or fifteen glasses of wine on other occasions. They do not tell their children that any use of alcohol is "bad" and then themselves proceed to consume several alcoholic beverages. They do not operate according to the dictate "do as I say, not as I do." They are able to discuss the matter of drinking with their children without becoming angry, defensive, or emotionally upset and they are able to maintain this stance on a very consistent basis. These parents respect their children and the life choices that their children make. They do not attempt to "force" their children to drink or abstain. However, they are able to actively and consistently explore the various dimensions of alcohol use with their children.

Responsible drinking does not diminish a parent or parent's basic sense of self-worth. Likewise, the children of responsible drinkers do not in any way feel threatened by their parent's use of alcohol. Their basic sense of self-worth and self-esteem is not diminished or eroded as a result of the drinking behaviors of a parent or parents. This is a very important point, as the children of alcoholics and alcohol abusers invariably feel emotionally upset as a result of the drinking behaviors of their addicted parent. The children of alcoholics also manifest a very damaged and lowered sense of self-worth as a result of parental drinking.

Parents who drink responsibly may or may not be globally responsible persons. Responsible people attempt to manage all areas of their lives in a responsible manner. Thus, it is important for parents to do their best to model responsible behaviors in all facets of their lives and interactions with their children—not only in the area of drinking and alcohol use!

Most parents question themselves about the responsible-irresponsible dimensions of many of their interactions with their children that involve drinking. For example, some parents wonder if it is appropriate and responsible to consume alcoholic beverages in the presence of their children. Most parents are at least somewhat apprehensive about drinking with their children—especially if their children are not legally old enough to drink. Is it responsible for a parent to permit his or her ten-year-old son to have a "sip" of beer or wine? The remainder of this chapter is devoted to an examination of these issues. Concrete guidelines are provided for the responsible parental management of each specific drinking situation.

PARENTAL DRINKING IN THE PRESENCE OF CHILDREN

Many parents and couples think nothing of consuming alcoholic beverages in front of their children. Others consciously decide not to imbibe in the presence of their children. Most drinking parents do not believe that it is harmful or inappropriate to imbibe in the presence of their children, especially when their children are very young. Drinking parents probably tend to be more concerned about the possible negative effects of drinking in front of their adolescent children. The basic reality of all situations involving a parent or parents consuming alcohol in the presence of children is that the drinking parent(s) is modeling and teaching his or her children a repertoire of alcohol use/drinking behaviors as well as pro-drinking attitudes, values, and beliefs. Some drinking parents may not consciously understand or recognize the various ramifications of drinking in front of their children. Nonetheless, all parents need to realize and accept that their personal styles of alcohol use and alcohol-drinking-oriented beliefs, values, and attitudes do effect and impact upon the alcohol-related behaviors, beliefs, attitudes, values and choices that their children develop.

With these important realities in mind, the following guidelines are provided for responsible parental drinking in the presence of children:

(1) Parental alcohol use is always limited in quantity and frequency,
(2) Parental consumption does not result in intoxication,
(3) Parental consumption does not result in cognitive, behavioral, affective, or familial relationship and communicative changes involving children, spouse, or the family system, and
(4) Parents are in general agreement about the issue of alcohol use in front of their children, and they are able to openly discuss drinking and alcohol use with each other and their children.

It is further suggested that parents maintain a style of consumption that does not involve ritualization and the deification of alcohol and drinking. Thus, parents who drink responsibly in the presence of their children might drink a glass of wine with the family dinner, they might consume a glass or two of champagne on New Year's Eve, or perhaps they may enjoy an alcoholic beverage with their neighbors. These parents do not drink "a cold beer" or "a few scotch and waters" each evening after "a hard day's work." They do not consume several alcoholic beverages or get "loaded" at family gatherings or social outings with neighbors, children, and friends. Their drinking behaviors do not somehow convey to their children or themselves a sense of magic, excitement, or an escape into the forbidden. Parents who drink responsibly feel comfortable discussing their drinking with each other and their children. They are able to communicate openly and honestly about alcohol use with their children. It is also important to note that these parents are not worried or apprehensive about their children observing them or being around them when they are drinking.

This last point is extremely important. I have observed that many drinking alcoholics and alcohol abusers are almost obsessed with the matter of not drinking in the presence of their children, spouses, and families. These drinkers hide their bottles, drink alone in the basement, garage, or camper, and they often refuse to talk about alcohol and drinking with their children and other family members. They seem to believe that by (1) keeping alcohol out of the home, (2) never drinking in the presence of their children, and (3) not verbally discussing their drinking or alcohol use, their personal alcohol dependence will be unknown to their children and family, and furthermore that these tactics will guard their children against becoming alcoholics. Some of these drinkers do 90 percent of their actual drinking in bars. They may stumble home each night for years at eight o'clock or after midnight, acutely intoxicated, smelling of alcohol, and behaviorally inappropriate and out of control. Yet, they continue to believe that their drinking or alcoholism has no impact on their children because their children do not ever actually observe them consuming alcohol. This belief system is obviously irrational, distorted, and steeped in self-deception and denial!

When alcoholics and problem drinkers consume alcoholic beverages in the presence of their children they are modeling inappropriate alcoholic behaviors, thinking, interacting, and communicating. These drinkers also model pathologic and alcoholic behaviors when they drink alone, in the basement or in bar settings. Their children become aware of the drinking at a young age, and every family member knows where Dad spends his evenings and they all are damaged by his "hidden" style of drinking.

It is very understandable why recovering alcoholics are so sensitive to the issue of drinking in front of children. The vast majority of these individuals drank alcoholically in front of their children. They not only consumed alcohol in the presence of their families, they also got drunk and behaved alcoholically on hundreds or thousands of occasions in front of their children and within the family milieu. Their drinking caused arguments and fights, marital and family discord, and feelings of guilt, embarrassment, anger, depression, confusion, fear and anxiety in their children and family members. Recovering parents know how their alcoholism has affected their children and families. They do not want to repeat their old alcoholic patterns of drinking, thinking, and behaving in the presence of their children. Indeed, they have made themselves alcoholically and psychologically sick vis-à-vis their drinking within the family system, and a major factor in recovery for many of these individuals is the need to repair relationships with children, spouses, and family members. Alcohol and drinking have caused many of their relationship difficulties with their children. Recovering people do not drink, but they remember very well how drinking in the presence of their children destroyed their personal sense of self-worth as well as the self-worth of their children.

Parents that are able to drink responsibly do not have extended histories of negative experiences involving alcohol and drinking in front of their children and families. This simple and basic reality explains why most parents who drink in moderation are not particularly worried or concerned about the issue of drinking in the presence of their children. Likewise, the children of these drinkers are not frightened or concerned about their parents' use of alcohol. They have not had the experience of being victims of parental alcohol-precipitated abuse or neglect. They are not concerned about their parents' alcohol use in their presence, and they do not anticipate that parental drinking will result in any type of negative consequences.

Finally, it is important for both parents to be in general agreement about drinking and alcohol use in the presence of their children. It is also essential that *both* parents be, if both parents are drinkers, responsible drinkers. These parents are able to openly and honestly share their beliefs, feelings, and attitudes about drinking with each other as well as with their children. They do not attempt to hide their alcohol use. They are not ambivalent about their personal use of alcohol, nor are they ambivalent about their spouse's use of alcohol.

DRINKING WITH CHILDREN

As indicated earlier, parents who do not have drinking problems tend not to be concerned or worried about drinking in front of their children. However, for most parents, the issue of drinking *with* children probably is far more complex and dissonance-provoking. Is it ever responsible for parents to drink with their children? If so, when? Perhaps some parents might even feel that it would be irresponsible for them not to introduce their children to drinking. Indeed, the issue of parents drinking with their children is controversial and provocative.

Most drinking parents do, in fact, imbibe with their children. Some of these parents may allow their children to "sip" an alcoholic beverage with them when they are quite young, while others refuse to drink with their children until they are adults. Regardless of the age or circumstances associated with parent-child drinking, research (NIAAA, 1978) indicates that six out of ten seventh-graders who report being drinkers had their initial drinking experiences with their parents on a special occasion. Early drinking experiences tend to occur at home and with parents and other family members. However, as children become older they tend to drink less with parents and more of their drinking takes place out of the home. For example, 50 percent of tenth-grade drinkers do their actual drinking in cars at night (Health Communications, 1978). These factors no doubt influence some parents in their decisions to drink with their children, allowing children to drink at home, and even advocating alcohol use in the home environment. Most parents realize that adolescents do the majority of their drinking outside of the home, with peers, and that peer pressure (Forrest, 1984) significantly affects adolescent patterns of alcohol consumption. Parents are generally apprehensive about adolescent alcohol and drug use, and they are particularly anxious when their sons or daughters imbibe in automobiles and out of the home milieu.

These issues can be very perplexing and confusing for parents as well as adolescents. Some parents seem to believe that they will be able to monitor and control the drinking behaviors of their sons and daughters if alcohol use is restricted to the home or takes place primarily between parents and children. Yet, most adolescents choose to drink with peers and away from the home. Adolescents also tend to be rebellious, impulsive, and they often equate their needs for independence and autonomy with the need to drink with peers rather than parents. No doubt, some parents as well as adolescents feel uncomfortable or guilty when they drink together.

In spite of the many conflicted issues that are associated with parents drinking *with* children, there are guidelines for the responsible management of this matter:

(1) Parental drinking with children can be responsible if the children have reached the legal drinking age; parental drinking with minors or underage children is illegal and irresponsible.
(2) Parent-child drinking interactions involve limited consumption on the part of all participants and these interactions are not frequent.
(3) Parents and children involved in alcohol use situations do not imbibe to the point of intoxication.
(4) Parent-child drinking interactions do not result in cognitive, behavioral, affective, or familial (parent[s]-child) relationship and communicative changes.

(5) Parents and children involved in these interactions are in general agreement about the issue of drinking together, and all parties are able to openly discuss their feelings and thoughts about alcohol use and drinking together.
(6) The adult children as well as the parents in these interactions are responsible drinkers and clearly not alcohol abusers, and
(7) Parents do not provide alcoholic beverages or a "safe drinking environment" for the friends and peers of their children.

When parents drink alcohol with their children they become very powerful and influential models who are actively condoning and reinforcing their children's drinking behaviors. These parents are clearly drinking role models and they overtly communicate to their children via their drinking behavior that it is okay to imbibe. They also give their children permission to drink, and they enable or reinforce their children's decisions about drinking and alcohol use.

Obviously, parents take on a great deal of responsibility when they choose to drink with their children. Drinking with children and family members is non-problematic when all parties are responsible drinkers and the guidelines presented earlier are maintained. Aside from being role models who reinforce alcohol use and give children permission to drink, parents who drink responsibly and follow these guidelines also teach their adult children a diversity of responsible behaviors that are specifically associated with drinking and alcohol use. This is a very important point. For example, these parents spend years teaching their children that it will be irresponsible and inappropriate for their children to drink with their own children before they reach the legal drinking age. Furthermore, when parents follow these guidelines for responsible drinking with early adult children, they are teaching and modeling globally non-abusive patterns of alcohol use.

Many parents may wonder if there are exceptions or flexible alternatives to these seven guidelines for parental alcohol use with children. The simple answer to this question is "yes." For example, a parent might ask if it is even responsible to drink an alcoholic beverage with an underage son or daughter? While it is clearly irresponsible to give a ten- or fifteen-year-old a beer or share an alcoholic beverage with a minor, it may not be irresponsible to allow an underage son or daughter to *taste* an alcoholic beverage. This is certainly a sensitive issue and one that "tests" the concept of gradients or shades of responsibility! Parents who allow their children to taste or sip from their alcoholic drinks on four or five occasions over a period of eighteen to twenty-one years are not irresponsible and they are not fostering the eventual irresponsible use of alcohol upon the part of their children.

The sensitive and controversial aspects of all forms of alcohol use with children are easily understood. Many alcoholics and severe alcohol abusers were given alcohol by their parents when they were very young children. Several of my alcoholic patients regularly drank to the point of acute and even stuperous intoxication *with* their parents when they were only ten to fourteen years old. Some of these patients reported that their parents "got them drunk" when they were three or four years old. Parents in these situations are grossly irresponsible and they actively contribute to the development of alcoholism and other forms of emotional pathology in their children. Most of these parents are also alcoholics and emotionally conflicted.

A very small number of "adults" also find it amusing to get their dogs, cats, or other pets intoxicated. Such acts are irresponsible, suggestive of immaturity, and illegal. Responsible drinkers do not engage in these acts.

Parent and adult-children drinking interactions that are managed responsibly by all parties involve the infrequent and limited use of alcohol, and these situations do not result in intoxication upon the part of any participant. Alcohol and drinking are not consistent or important components in these parent-child interactions. In fact, responsible parents teach their children that it is not important or necessary for children to drink or use alcohol in *any* social situation. These parents actively reinforce the non-alcohol use choice as well as the responsible drinking choice in their ongoing interactions with their children!

Parents and adult children who drink together responsibly are not ambivalent and conflicted about the issue of imbibing on a familial basis. The parents as well as children in these situations are not upset or at loggerheads over the reality of alcohol use. Drinking does not in any way errode the configuration of family-adult-children-parental relationships, and each family member is able to openly discuss his or her perceptions and feelings about familial alcohol use if such a discussion is needed or appropriate.

There are many family situations in which both parents and *most* of the adult children are moderate drinkers or non-drinkers. However, when one or more of the adult children in any family are irresponsible drinkers, it is irresponsible for *any* family member to drink with the family member who has a drinking problem. This situation also applies to parents! It is irresponsible and inappropriate for a parent who is a responsible drinker to imbibe together with his or her spouse if the spouse is an alcoholic or alcohol abuser. Likewise, it is irresponsible and inappropriate for adult children to choose to drink with a parent who is unable to drink responsibly! Thus, guideline six applies to *all* parents and children that use alcohol together.

Finally, parents who use alcohol responsibly do not reinforce the drinking behaviors of peers and friends of their adult children by purchasing liquor, "throwing keg parties," or in other ways providing drinking environments for these people. The parents of some high school students do purchase beer for their sons and daughters as well as other teenagers. Some of these parents allow their children and friends to drink alcohol in their homes. They may actually "throw a kegger" for their children and other teenagers. These transactions are inappropriate, irresponsible, and illegal. Parents who purchase alcoholic beverages for their teenage sons and daughters and their teenage peers are also taking a *tremendous* legal risk: the risk of being sued. Whenever an adult purchases or provides alcoholic beverages for a minor he or she is not only in violation of the law, this person is legally liable for any behavior or outcome that is associated with the minor's use of the alcohol which the adult purchased or provided! Ultimately, responsibility is shared in all situations where one person provides another with alcoholic beverages and encourages drinking. Thus, *both* parties are responsible. If a parent gives his or her son several alcoholic drinks, regardless of the son's age, the parent and the son must assume shared responsibility for any behavior, event, or outcome that is associated with the son's alcohol use.

It is apparent that many risks can be associated with situations that involve parents and children drinking together. Yet, many parents do drink with their adult children on an infrequent basis and these parent-child drinking situations do not result in problems. Parents and adult children can, in fact, drink responsibly *together!* However, there are a number of very important prerequisite guidelines and requirements that need to be met in order for parent-child drinking interactions to be responsible and non-problematic. *All* participants in these situations must consistently act and behave in accord with these guidelines. Common sense and good judgment also need to be exercised in any situation involving alcohol use.

When parents are able to use alcohol responsibly they axiomatically tend to use alcohol responsibly in the presence of their children and with their adult children. Drinking and alcohol use constitute very small components of the processes of living, experiencing, sharing, and growing through life as parents and children; when parents and adult children eventually drink together responsibly, shared drinking experiences between parents and children are no more important, significant, or meaningful than sharing a hamburger.

SUMMARY

This chapter includes an examination of the concept of responsible parental alcohol use. Guidelines for responsible parental alcohol use are provided throughout the chapter. Parents who drink responsibly serve as role models for their children. These parents drink in moderation, they are open and communicative about their use of alcohol, they do not drink to the point of intoxication, and they actively teach their children about responsible alcohol use. The drinking behaviors of these parents do not change or diminish their basic sense of self-worth, and their children do not experience self-worth changes as a result of parental alcohol use. Parents who are responsible drinkers consistently teach their children that alcohol use is not an important or necessary component of human interaction. They also teach their children that it is appropriate and acceptable to choose not to use alcohol. The basic reality of all situations involving a parent or parents consuming alcohol in the presence of children is that the drinking parent(s) is modeling and teaching his or her children a repertoire of alcohol use/drinking behaviors as well as pro-drinking attitudes, values, and beliefs.

The guidelines for responsible parental alcohol use in the presence of children encompass such issues as frequency of use, open communication about drinking, quantity of use and intoxication, and parental agreement-dissonance surrounding alcohol use. It is irresponsible for parents to in any way abuse or misuse alcohol. Parents who are able to drink responsibly do not worry about their children observing them consume an alcoholic beverage.

Some parents feel that it is irresponsible to drink in front of their children. Indeed, many drinking alcoholics "hide" their drinks or bottles, drink only in bars, or drink alone in the basement. Some parents may also believe that it is inappropriate to discuss alcohol and drug use/abuse with their children. It is my feeling that children know when their parents are alcoholics or severe alcohol abusers in spite of whether these parents drink in the presence of their children or not. Children in alcoholic families are damaged in myriad ways by their parents' alcohol dependence, and it matters very little where the parent or parents actually do their drinking. Furthermore, all parents need to actively and consistently communicate with their children about alcohol use and other drugs.

The anxieties and ambivalence that recovering alcoholics experience over the issue of alcohol use in the presence of children are discussed.

Drinking with children presents both parents and children with various controversial and provocative dilemmas as well as a plethora of responsibilities. Research findings indicate that most children have their initial drinking experiences with their parents in their home environment. Adolescents tend to drink with peers rather than parents, and most of their alcohol consumption occurs outside the home. When parents do imbibe with their children it is important that they as well as their children adhere to the guidelines delineated in this chapter. The guidelines for responsible parent-adult children alcohol use include such issues as age, emotional maturity, communicative skills, prior personal and familial drinking history, and social-interpersonal factors pertaining to *all* parties involving alcohol use interactions.

Parents need to be fully cognizant of the various responsibilities they assume when they choose to imbibe with their adult children. Alcohol use with children and family members can be non-problematic when *all* parties in these situations are responsible drinkers and the guidelines for responsible parent-adult children alcohol use are followed.

Finally, it is grossly irresponsible for parents to "get drunk" or abuse alcohol with their children. This is true regardless of the child's age. It's also irresponsible for parents to provide alcoholic beverages for their children's friends and for social functions that include minors.

Parents who drink responsibly also consistently communicate to their adult children that it is okay—that it is responsible, to choose not to drink or use alcohol in many, if not most, social situations! Alcohol use between parents and adult-children can be a very unimportant matter when managed responsibly by all parties in all situations!

Chapter 7

WHEN TEENAGERS DRINK: CAN TEEN ALCOHOL USE BE RESPONSIBLE?

FACING FACTS: MOST TEENS ARE DRINKERS!

As indicated in Chapter 3, teenagers typically begin to "experiment" with alcohol between the ages of twelve and fourteen. Indeed, teen alcohol use steadily increases between the ages of thirteen and nineteen. More teenagers become alcohol users as they enter the late teens, and teen drinkers also generally tend to drink more frequently as they become older. For example, about 60 percent of fourteen-year-olds are drinkers, while over 90 percent of eighteen-year-olds drink. Well over 90 percent of college students in the age range of seventeen to nineteen are alcohol users!

Many of the devastating consequences of teen alcohol use were also outlined in Chapter 3. Teenage drinking is consistently associated with family conflict, unwanted pregnancy and sexual difficulties, automobile accidents and fatalities, legal problems, school and academic problems, drug abuse and addiction, suicide, and peer conflicts. Nonetheless, the fact remains that many, if not most, teenagers consume alcoholic beverages! Furthermore, American teenagers have been drinkers for several decades. There is no reason to believe that teens will suddenly discontinue their historic pattern of being consumers of alcohol!

There are a plethora of factors that explain or partially explain why teenagers use alcohol. American teenagers certainly grow up in a culture which is alcohol and other drug oriented! In general, Americans are drinkers. Furthermore, alcohol is relatively cheap, readily accessible, socially acceptable, and "fast acting." The gateway to late adolescence and early adulthood in America has long been framed in alcohol use and heavy drinking. Traditionally, we seem to have expected teens to "sow their oats" with John Barleycorn! In addition to the many negative relationships involving teens and alcohol use, no doubt many teenagers believe that they are able to derive some form or degree of positive benefit from drinking. Some young drinkers (Orford, 1985) report that drinking helps them relax, feel more comfortable with others, and establish closer ties with a peer group. Finally, teens are consistently and continually bombarded with media messages that reinforce drinking and alcohol use. When all of these factors are taken into account in combination with the realization that we are all biologically addictive (Forrest, 1984), it is not at all surprising that the vast majority of teenagers are drinkers. Conversely, perhaps it is amazing that all teenagers are not alcohol users!

When parents, educators, health providers, law enforcement personnel, the clergy, and communities began to accept the fact that most teens are drinkers they begin to be confronted with a diversity of confusing and difficult questions and realities. Indeed, it is relatively easy to understand why mom and dad often deny the stark reality of a son or daughter's drinking or drug abuse. It may seem easier to deny, avoid, or cover up these issues. Parents understandably want to tell their friends "Thank God, Roger would never do that!" Yet, as we all know too well, the price and consequences of parental denial and avoidance can be tragic when it comes to the matter of adolescent drinking.

CAN TEENAGERS DRINK RESPONSIBLY?

When parents, educators, health providers, and others who are interested and concerned about teenage alcohol use begin to accept the fact that most teens are drinkers, they are immediately confronted with the question or dilemma of responsible teenage drinking. Can teenage alcohol use in fact be responsible? No doubt, many parents and others believe that virtually all teen alcohol use is irresponsible. The question of responsible teenage drinking is indeed thorny and conflicted for all of us.

It was suggested in Chapter 3 that most parents, educators, and health providers clearly agree that *any* drinking upon the part of a fourteen- or fifteen-year-old is irresponsible. Yet, the alcohol use of an eighteen- or nineteen-year-old may be more difficult to evaluate from the dichotomous perspective of responsible vs. irresponsible. While many states have recently raised their legal drinking age from eighteen or nineteen to twenty-one, it is still "legal" for teens to consume some alcoholic beverages in some states. As elucidated in Chapter 4, all forms of responsible behavior involve "moral, *legal*, and mental accountability."

The simple fact is that any alcohol use upon the part of a legally defined "minor" constitutes an irresponsible act. Thus, if a particular state legislates that one must be twenty-one years of age in order to "legally" consume alcoholic beverages, it is clearly irresponsible for any person under the age of twenty-one to consume alcohol or even attempt to procure an alcoholic beverage in that state. Likewise, it is both irresponsible and illegal for any person or business establishment to sell, provide, or distribute alcoholic beverages to a person under the age of twenty-one (a "minor") in such a state! Underage minors who consume alcoholic beverages or attempt to procure alcoholic beverages are behaving irresponsibly and illegally as are adults or businesses who sell or distribute ethanol to minors.

The age-based criteria for assessing the responsible-irresponsible nature of adolescent alcohol use can be very clear-cut but also dissonance-provoking. For example, if the legal drinking age in one state is twenty-one but only eighteen in an adjacent state, many eighteen- to twenty-year-olds can be expected to cross state lines where this is practical in order to drink legally in the state that has the younger age requirement for alcohol consumption. These situations can prove to be very perplexing for parents and law enforcement personnel as well as teenage drinkers. Consider the various legal and parental considerations that might be associated with situations involving teenagers who drink legally in one state at the age of eighteen or nineteen and then return immediately after drinking to their home in a state that has a legal drinking age requirement of twenty-one! Issues associated with age requirements for purchase of alcoholic beverages, sale of alcoholic beverages, drinking and driving implications, and parental and teen drinking conflicts can be expected in these situations.

State and local laws that govern the sales of alcoholic beverages, distribution of alcoholic beverages, nature of drinking establishments, hours of serving alcoholic beverages, and so forth are also issues that can contribute to the dissonance surrounding teen alcohol use. Many adult drinkers are even confused about the various laws and rules that govern alcohol use in different counties or different states. Indeed, the global variability in the laws that govern drinking and alcohol use can be dissonance provoking for non-drinkers as well as drinkers of all ages.

Two or three decades ago many states seem to have favored younger age requirements for alcohol consumption. Several states required that teens be only eighteen years of age in order to legally drink beer. More recently, the federal government has motivated a number of states to raise their legal drinking age requirement to twenty-one. Historically, many Americans have believed that males in particular should be able to drink legally at age eighteen because this is the approximate age for induction into the armed forces. The general logic that supported this belief system involved the notion that men who are old enough to serve their country or perhaps even die for their country should be old enough to consume alcoholic beverages! Americans have also tended to believe that human beings become truly responsible for their actions between the ages of eighteen and twenty-one, and thus we legally permit individuals in this age group to drink, vote, live outside the primary family system, marry, work, and so forth.

It is important to keep in mind that the age dimension of the issue of responsible and irresponsible teenage alcohol use can be the simplest and least confusing aspect of this matter. When the focus of the question of responsible vs. irresponsible adolescent alcohol use is shifted to include the concepts and general parameters of responsibility and responsible and irresponsible drinking behavior that were delineated in Chapters 2 and 4, this issue becomes much more controversial and complicated. In order to avoid excessive redundancy, the basic concepts of responsibility and responsible drinking can be summarized as:

(1) Responsible behavior involves being able to satisfy one's basic needs in a rational manner that does not deprive others of the ability to meet their basic needs. Responsible behaviors and responsible living contribute to the development of a positive sense of self-esteem and facilitate a feeling of worth and value to others. Responsible behavior is based upon the concepts of honesty, fairness, truth, and personal integrity. Responsible acts involve moral, legal, and mental accountability.

(2) Responsible drinking is consuming alcohol in a manner that is in no way injurious to the psychological, interpersonal, physical, moral, legal, or spiritual well-being of the drinker, society, or other people.

The various parameters of irresponsible alcohol use were also explored in Chapter 4. As noted, in a basic sense irresponsible drinking is the converse of responsible drinking.

These concepts of responsibility, responsible alcohol use, and irresponsible alcohol use can be applied to the drinking and alcohol-related behaviors of any teenage drinker. This is true regardless of the actual age of the adolescent drinker.

It was also suggested in earlier chapters that responsible drinkers tend to imbibe on an infrequent basis, they drink in moderation and do not drink to the point of intoxication, their alcohol use does not result in detrimental cognitive, behavioral, affective, or global personality changes, and their drinking does not impact negatively upon their personal sense of self-esteem or deprive others of their ability to meet basic needs and maintain a good sense of self-worth. Obviously, these drinkers do not in any way behave irresponsibly, immorally, or illegally as a result of imbibing.

Consider the various precepts of responsible alcohol use as they might be applied to a hypothetical fourteen-year-old female drinker. Is our adolescent a responsible drinker if her drinking behavior does not interfere with her ability to satisfy her basic needs in a rational manner that does not deprive others of the ability to meet their basic needs? What do we think about her drinking behavior if she rarely drinks—perhaps only once or twice a year? Perhaps she has never imbibed to the point of intoxication and limits her consumption to one or two alcoholic beverages per drinking occasion. How would we evaluate her use of ethanol if she does *not* experience "problems" as a result of drinking—school or family problems, legal problems, health problems, interpersonal or peer conflicts, self-worth problems? Perhaps her parents even actively condone her drinking; they believe that it is okay for teenagers to drink as long as they imbibe in a "responsible" and controlled fashion, and their daughter has repeatedly demonstrated to them that she can do these very things. How do we assess these young drinkers? Perhaps they are responsible drinkers?

Parents, teenagers, physicians and various other health service providers, educators, and others are faced with these questions and dilemmas on a daily basis. They are personal, professional, and social issues that all of us must deal with on a regular basis. Thousands of parents are confronted with a diversity of issues associated with their teenage sons' and daughters' use of alcohol on a *daily* basis! All too often, teachers and school administrative personnel must make important decisions that are based upon their personal beliefs or values that are associated with these questions. For example, if a teacher smells alcohol on the breath of a student but the student does not appear to be acutely intoxicated, what action does the teacher take? Finally, young drinkers must continually confront themselves with these questions and dilemmas. Their parents, peers, and significant others also bombard them with these matters. Most teenagers are faced with the choices of "doing" drugs, consuming alcoholic beverages, or saying no to alcohol and drug use everytime they attend a party or social function. Likewise, the parents of many teens worry about the alcohol-drug choices that their children will make everytime they attend a party, go out on a date, or leave for a rock concert.

In spite of all the confusion and caveats surrounding the question of responsible alcohol use upon the part of teenagers who are legally minors, the basic fact remains: it is illegal and thus *categorically irresponsible* for any minor to consume, purchase, or distribute alcoholic beverages. This is the bottom-line reality with regard to the question of responsible teen drinking.

Most adults realize that a sizeable segment of underage teenage drinkers rarely abuse alcohol. Yet, some adults somehow seem to overlook the fact that these drinkers are in reality irresponsible drinkers because they actually violate several laws everytime they choose to imbibe. Perhaps this matter touches upon the growing American style of thinking, which in effect says illegal or irresponsible acts are only "bad" when the violator is caught or proven guilty. This pervasive belief system or style of thinking reinforces the idea that it is okay or acceptable to "bend" or even break laws, social rules, and mores, but it is not acceptable to get caught engaging in these illegal activities. Some parents and other authority figures actually reinforce this style of thinking and behaving when they tell underage drinkers "it's okay, just don't get caught" or "it's alright as long as I don't know about it." In recent years many parents have engaged in this type of enabling behavior by demanding that their teens do not "drink and drive." Sometimes the crazy message behind this parental message is "any drinking or form of alcohol-related behavior is acceptable, except drinking and driving!"

Thus, it is very clear that even if our hypothetical fourteen-year-old girl is able to consume alcoholic beverages from time to time without experiencing problems in any of the clinically oriented areas that we have used to define alcohol abuse and alcoholism, she is nonetheless a *girl—legally* a minor and hence an irresponsible drinker.

Very often it is helpful for parents, educators, mental health workers, and teens to remain focused upon the basic and fundamental realities of life. The law is the law! It can be relatively easy for all of us to forget, bend, or distort the basic reality that one must reach a specific age in order to drink legally and responsibly. Twenty is not twenty-one and fourteen is certainly not twenty-one!

It is important to also realize that *most* teenagers clearly understand that it is illegal and irresponsible for them to imbibe and use other mood-altering chemicals. In spite of this realization, most teenagers continue to episodically abuse alcohol. All too frequently young people in part persist in their patterns of alcohol and drug abuse because parents and other authority figures are unable to consistently set rules and limits that convey the message "these behaviors are irresponsible and unacceptable." Teenagers and their parents tend to be ambivalent about alcohol use. Teens need and want parents to help them define or set limits. The struggles that adolescents experience vis-à-vis separating from the family, individuating, rebelling, and acting-out can be viewed as attempts to internally define or clarify limits, boundaries, and responsibility. Teens need to feel that they are responsible, worthwhile persons, and these needs are reinforced via parent-teen interactions that consistently reinforce responsible teen behaviors.

Parental and authority-figure ambivalence that is associated with setting and reinforcing alcohol use limits can be very confusing to teenagers. Teenagers easily interpret parental "mixed messages" about alcohol use as permission to drink. Parents and teens need to be very clear about the limits and dimensions of responsible alcohol use. These issues need to be openly discussed and explored by teens and their parents in an ongoing, consistent, flexible manner.

Parental and authority figure flexibility in discussing and setting limits with adolescents does not preempt the need for consistent reinforcement of basic rules and responsibilities. This matter is rather paradoxical in nature. Yet, the bottom line is that relatively specific rules and regulations govern or shape most of our social behaviors. For example, fifteen-year-olds cannot vote in a presidential election. Ten-year-olds cannot enlist in the army or obtain a driver's license. With regard to alcohol and drug use, parents and teens need to be open and flexible enough to consistently communicate about these issues, but parents and authority figures also need to be firm enough to set, reinforce, and enforce the rules and limits associated with drinking and drug use. Parents need to help teens establish and internalize responsible attitudes, beliefs, and behaviors that involve alcohol and alcohol use.

A final issue of critical importance that must be addressed when we consider the problem of responsible teen alcohol use involves the many devastating consequences of teen alcohol use. Adolescent drinking and intoxication are the primary or secondary causes of thousands of injuries, accidents, automobile wrecks, family problems, suicides, homicides, legal problems, and school problems. Furthermore, teen drinking results in these myriad problems on a minute-to-minute basis, every day and hour of the year. The costs of irresponsible adolescent drinking are truly immeasurable! These "costs" involve human emotions, dollars and cents, physical suffering and pain, lives, and time.

A few months ago I was lecturing at the Family Recovery Center of Grand Island Memorial Hospital in Grand Island, Nebraska. By chance I had the fortune of listening to a very good friend and colleague, Jim DeWitt, M.D., discuss the "Disease Concept of Alcoholism." During his dynamic and emotionally moving presentation, Doctor DeWitt pointed out to the audience that *alcoholism* and severe alcohol abuse rarely kill or injure teenagers—to the contrary, the great killer and maimer of teenagers is usually "a few beers." I couldn't agree more with Doctor DeWitt. Most teenagers are simply unable to consistently drink responsibly. The majority of teens are episodic alcohol abusers. They are not alcohol-dependent, and most of these young people will eventually become responsible alcohol users—if they live or are not seriously injured as a result of their periodic alcohol abuse. This is the problem! Irresponsible alcohol use, not chronic alcoholism or drug dependence, kills and injures thousands of teens each year. Indeed, over seven thousand teenagers are killed while drinking and driving each year. Think about the pain and tragedy that are caused by "a couple of beers" or "a few beers" each day in this country.

Just as parents and significant others can teach and reinforce the parameters of responsible alcohol use with their teenage sons and daughters, so can teens help each other with these issues. Teen alcohol and drug abuse involve social issues that affect all of us. As *responsible human beings* all of us share the various responsibilities that are associated with extinguishing alcohol abuse, alcoholism, and chemical dependency.

SUMMARY

Parents, educators, health service providers, the clergy, law enforcement personnel, and teens themselves—indeed, all of us need to face facts! Most teenagers are drinkers, and a significant percentage of teens abuse a diversity of other mood-altering chemicals. Over 90 percent of late teens drink alcoholic beverages with some degree of regularity. Furthermore, there are no immediate reasons to support the hypothesis that significant numbers of teens will stop drinking or drink less frequently and less abusively in the immediate future.

Several of the factors that cause or reinforce teen alcohol use were briefly outlined in this chapter. When parents and significant others begin to accept the various realities of teen drinking, they are immediately confronted with the question of responsible teen alcohol use. Can adolescent alcohol use in fact be responsible?

It was emphasized throughout this chapter that any alcohol use upon the part of a legally defined "minor" is clearly irresponsible. However, the chameleon-like dimensions and continuum nature of the concept of responsibility seem to make it more difficult to assess the alcohol use behaviors of eighteen- and nineteen-year-olds. This confusion is particularly apparent and understandable in situations that involve older adolescents who are clearly not alcoholics or alcohol abusers. These teens may be infrequent drinkers. They do not lose control of their drinking, and they meet the various other parameters of responsible behavior and responsible alcohol use that have been delineated in earlier chapters. Yet, the "bottom-line" reality in these cases is very simple: it is irresponsible for *anyone* to engage in any behavior that is in violation of the law!

It was also pointed out in this chapter that most teenagers know that it is irresponsible and illegal for them to consume alcoholic beverages and take other mood-altering chemicals. Many teens, in part, drink and take drugs because their parents and other authority figures are unable to consistently set and enforce the limits and rules that apply to the use of these substances. Teens and parents as well as society are ambivalent about alcohol use. Many parents seem to be unable to tell their underage children that it is inappropriate and irresponsible to drink. Some parents are so conflicted themselves that they either deny or simply aren't aware of their teenage son or daughter's drinking and drugging. Many teens are unable to say no to alcohol and drugs because they fear peer rejection; they need to feel accepted and valued by their peers, and such acceptance may be intricately linked to imbibing and using drugs with their peers. Finally, authority figures such as the police, educators, and even family physicians are ambivalent about communicating openly and honestly with teens and their parents about drinking and drugs because they (1) lack information specific to these areas, (2) fear the potential consequences of such dialogue, (3) feel they don't know what actions to take, or (4) simply feel overwhelmed by the magnitude of these problems and have in essence "given up" as a result of their feelings of futility.

Consider the following situation. Police officers here in Colorado Springs have experienced a great deal of personal anxiety, fear, frustration, and concern about their historic inability to take some form of action with teens that they have picked up who were acutely intoxicated. Until recently, our community had no legal plan of action or facility where these teens could be taken for detoxification and treatment. Therefore, police officers routinely drove these teens around in their police cruisers, bought them coffee, provided a safe environment until they "sobered up," and then took them home or simply let them go. The officers in these cases took many personal risks. Some of these teens were "runaways," many of their parents were also "drunks," or their parents were simply not concerned about their children's behavior and whereabouts. How many hundreds of other communities are there throughout the United States that have not begun to face these problems and realities?

The costs of irresponsible teen drinking are enormous. As noted in this chapter, the greater killers and maimers of teens are "a few beers" and "recreational drug use." Teenagers as well as parents, educators, behavioral scientists, and communities need to dedicate themselves to the various processes that are needed to eliminate the problems of *human* substance abuse and addiction.

Chapter 8

DRINKING AND DRIVING

AN AMERICAN TRADITION

Americans have a long tradition of drinking and driving. We are largely responsible for the development of the automobile, superhighways, and rapid transportation. Perhaps it is only fitting that we should also be the innovators of drinking and driving. American's consume alcohol while driving automobiles, motorcycles, speedboats, bicycles, heavy equipment, airplanes, and trains. Virtually all modes of transportation in this country somehow involve alcohol use.

Many Americans measure distance or miles by number of drinks. Instead of conceptualizing the distance between Denver, Colorado, and Kansas City, Missouri as five hundred miles, these people perceive the "distance" between these cities as a case of beer or a quart of vodka. A patient of mine referred to the time and traffic conditions between his office and home as usually "three-drink traffic."

Prior to the mid-seventies most Americans were unconcerned or unaware of the dangers that are associated with drinking and driving. The jukeboxes of the late fifties and sixties were filled with tunes that extolled the virtues of drinking and driving. Songs like "6-Pak To Go" and the "One for the Road" mentality reinforced attitudes, beliefs, and values that were pro-alcohol-automobile use oriented. Most people who grew up in this era were simply unaware of the risks of drinking and operating a vehicle, and the media, law enforcement, and social organizations did not consistently attempt to overtly educate and inform the general public of these risks. Perhaps basic ignorance and misunderstanding rather than collective denial contributed to most of the drinking and driving that occurred in this country prior to the mid-seventies.

During the past few years, Americans have begun to wake up and realize the devastating consequences that are associated with alcohol use and driving. Indeed, we are now exposed to television and radio messages that graphically and realistically depict those consequences. Law enforcement officers and the judicial system have begun to arrest and prosecute large numbers of drinking drivers throughout the country. Attorneys are finding it progressively more difficult to get their DUI clients "off the hook," and it is becoming harder to get judges to either "look the other way" or "slap" these offenders on the wrists. Americans are beginning to fear the drinking driver. We are also beginning to perceive the drinking driver as a very dangerous person—a potential murderer!

In short, the American tradition of drinking and driving is under increasing attack. Fortunately, this tradition is literally dying. Mothers Against Drunk Drivers (MADD) is a recent organization that has actively facilitated several social and legal changes that pertain to alcohol use and driving. The MADD organization was literally started by a mother whose daughter was killed by an intoxicated driver. Students Against Drunk Drivers (SADD) and several similar organizations have evolved over recent years. These social organizations have actively helped develop new laws and legislation that apply to drinking drivers. These organizations have also raised our collective awareness of the realities of drinking and driving.

An awareness of the devastating consequences of drinking and driving leads to the question of responsible alcohol use and driving. As people begin to realize and accept the fact that alcohol and driving do not "mix," they are ultimately confronted with such questions as "Is it responsible to consume *any* amount of ethanol and then drive?" or "Is it responsible to consume a certain amount of alcohol and then drive?" It is important for the reader to consider the following consequences of drinking and driving before attempting to formulate answers pertaining to the matter of responsible alcohol use and driving.

CONSEQUENCES OF DRINKING AND DRIVING

It is difficult to know precisely how many drivers in the United States consume alcoholic beverages before or while they are behind the wheel of an automobile. No doubt, many people engage in drinking and driving behaviors on an infrequent basis. Most drivers would agree that it is illegal, irresponsible, and dangerous to drive while *drunk.* However, it is logical to expect that many or perhaps most people believe that it is not irresponsible to operate a vehicle if one is not *legally* intoxicated. The issue of "legal intoxication" is confusing to many people, as they do not know what this concept entails. Some believe that a person must consume several alcoholic beverages in a short period of time in order to be "legally intoxicated," while others may believe that one alcoholic drink may result in meeting this criterion.

In spite of the confusion and lack of general understanding surrounding these issues, most Americans do realize that drinking and driving does result in myriad negative consequences for thousands of people every day of every year. Consider the following consequences of drinking and driving:

(1) Drinking drivers are *25 times* more likely to have accidents than sober or non-drinking drivers.
(2) Drinking is a primary causative factor in half of all highway traffic fatalities.
(3) Approximately *twenty-five thousand people are killed each year* on our highways by drinking drivers.
(4) Approximately 25,000 people have been killed each year on our highways by drinking drivers *every year* for over two decades—a total of 500,000 deaths!
(5) Nearly 500,000 people are injured on our highways each year by intoxicated drivers, and
(6) Drunk driving is the leading single cause of death among young drivers between the ages of 16 and 24; some *7,000* teens have been killed while drinking and driving each year for nearly two decades!

These facts are real. The consequences of drinking and driving are devastating. Yet, many Americans choose to ignore these realities or they simply do not believe the "statistics." Unfortunately, human beings tend to deny or minimize the significance of events that do not touch them personally. Perhaps the "numbers game" of experience is beginning to catch up with the American collective. The hundreds of thousands of parents, spouses, children, and loved ones of the 250,000 people who have been killed on our highways during the past decade are beginning to make "legal and social noises"—and they are starting to be heard.

These facts are really just the tip of the iceberg with regard to drinking and accidents. Heavy drinkers and alcoholics are seven times more likely than non-drinkers to be killed in various kinds of accidents. Snowmobile, boating, motorcycle, and fatal accidents in the home are frequently alcohol-related. In fact, alcohol is a causative factor in over 50 percent of all accidental deaths!

Many drivers become murderers every day—as a result of drinking and driving. Countless numbers of people also become victims of drinking drivers each day. Yet, we have remained largely unconcerned about these realities for twenty to thirty years. Most of us have been more emotionally concerned and ego-involved in the reality of losing nearly 59,000 American GI's in Vietnam over a ten-year period. Think about this for a minute. Intoxicated drivers killed some 250,000 *Americans* on *our* highways during this same ten-year period! Perhaps it is somehow more acceptable for Americans to kill, injure, or slaughter other Americans?

How Drinking Affects Driving

It is important for all of us to understand the fundamentals of drinking and driving—how alcohol use actually affects our driving behaviors. First of all, alcohol is absorbed very rapidly by the mucous membranes of the stomach and upper portion of the small intestine and then rapidly carried to the brain. Other foods and beverages must be digested before they are absorbed by the body. Alcohol does not have to be digested in order to be absorbed by the body systems, and thus alcohol quickly affects behavior, thinking, coordination, and psychomotor skills. Alcohol is a central nervous system (CNS) depressant and therefore slows the drinker's reflexes, thinking, and judgment. The chemical makeup of alcohol is very similar to ether and affects the drinker like an anesthetic.

Many people do not know how much alcohol they must consume in order to be legally considered driving while intoxicated. The laws of most states specify that a driver is intoxicated when his or her percent of alcohol in the blood is .10 or above. Many states consider drivers to be "legally impaired" when their BACs (blood alcohol concentration) are .05 or above. What do these percentages actually mean in terms of numbers of alcoholic drinks consumed, specific beverages consumed, and time involved in drinking? Several factors must be taken into account when we answer questions such as these.

In general, if you consume three beers or two "mixed drinks" containing a total of three ounces of 86-proof ethanol or three 4-ounce glasses of wine within a period of about one-and-one-half hours, your BAC (the amount of alcohol in your blood) is approximately .05 percent. This is enough alcohol in the blood to be considered impaired. If a person consumes about four mixed drinks in one-and-one-half hours, his or her BAC will be .10 or over. This level of intoxication in combination with driving is generally referred to as "drunk driving." Colorado drivers who are arrested with a BAC of .15 or above must surrender their driver's licenses to the arresting officer, as this level of intoxication is felt to produce extreme driving risks. A lethal ethanol dose is generally within a BAC range of .35–.45.

It is also important to know that it takes a 150–160-pound man at least one hour to metabolize one ounce of 86 proof liquor. Thus, drinking several alcoholic beverages over an extended period of time cumulatively raises the drinker's BAC. If a drinker consumes ten ounces of ethanol it will take approximately ten hours for his body to completely metabolize this amount of alcohol.

The amount of time that elapses between drinking ethanol, number of drinks consumed, and driving is crucial in determining if a person is driving while impaired or intoxicated. For example, if a person attended a party for a period of four hours and consumed two ounces of ethanol (2 mixed drinks or 2.5 beers) during this time and then drove home, he or she would not be *legally* guilty of driving while impaired. However, if this same person consumed eight ounces of ethanol in the same period of time his or her BAC will be about .08 and thus would result in a driving while impaired or under the influence arrest. In this case, it must be remembered that the drinker's body would only be able to metabolize one ounce of alcohol per hour—or one half the amount that was consumed in the period of four hours. The cumulative effects of drinking can literally "sneak up" on the drinker!

A drinker's size, weight, and amount or type of food in the stomach can all influence degree of intoxication and BAC level. A 100-pound woman may be significantly impaired after consuming three 4–5-ounce glasses of wine in a two-hour period of time. However, a 250-pound male would need to consume five or six glasses of wine in order to reach the same level of impairment. Food in the stomach delays and to some extent dilutes the absorption of alcohol. Thus, people who drink on an "empty stomach" literally become intoxicated and impaired more quickly than those who have eaten prior to or with drinking.

A diversity of psychological factors may also affect an individual's response to drinking. For example, the environment in which an individual imbibes may influence how much or how fast he or she consumes alcoholic beverages. The actual psychological "set" of the drinker may influence self-perceived degree of intoxication and social behaviors following drinking. It is important to remember that the social appearance of being intoxicated or self-perceptions pertaining to degree of intoxication can be very misleading. Many times people do not act drunk and they do not perceive themselves as being intoxicated. Yet, in fact, they are *legally* impaired or intoxicated if their BACs are above .05 percent. Somewhat paradoxically, many chronic alcoholics do not appear to be intoxicated when in reality their BAC's are above .20! This is why the law requires that drivers who are *suspected* of drinking and driving must take a "breathalizer" examination or blood test within a specific interval of time following arrest.

Perhaps it will be helpful for the reader to bear in mind that by consuming only three beers in a period of one-and-one-half to two hours (.05 BAC) a person's driving abilities are impaired in the following areas:

(1) total driving impairment is 25–50 percent,
(2) reaction time is slowed between 15 and 25 percent,
(3) recovery time for headlight glare is 10 to 30 seconds longer,
(4) peripheral vision is decreased,
(5) visual acuity can be reduced by up to one-third, and
(6) perception and judgments pertaining to speed and distance are impaired.

Impaired psychomotor skills, reduced eye-hand coordination, poor thinking and judgment, and perceptual defects occur as a result of consuming only two or three alcoholic beverages in a relatively short period of time! These impairments are extremely dangerous to the drinking driver as well as any other person he or she encounters while operating a motor vehicle.

A diversity of psychological and emotional impairments can also occur following drinking. These psychological impairments contribute to the dangerous and potentially risky practice of drinking and driving. The drinking or intoxicated driver tends to manifest an unrealistic sense of driving competency. These drivers often take unnecessary risks on the highway and they tend to talk a great deal while driving. They may also become angry and emotionally upset while driving. Very often it is the acutely intoxicated spouse at the party who *demands* to drive home—this person attempts to emotionally convince his wife that he is not "drunk," that he has "never had a wreck," and that he "will drive very carefully." Such a person manifests *all* of the alcohol-facilitated impairments that have just been discussed! It is important to fully realize that people in these situations are indeed very dangerous; thousands of these individuals become highway murderers every year in our country!

The Responsible-Irresponsible Dimensions of Drinking and Driving

As indicated earlier in this chapter, a driver is considered to be legally impaired when his or her blood alcohol concentration (BAC) is .05 percent or higher. This level of blood alcohol concentration is generally reached after an individual has consumed three alcoholic beverages within a period of about one-and-one-half hours. The laws of nearly all states specify that people who drive while having BACs of .10 or above are "driving while *intoxicated.*"

Thus, according to the criteria that were used in Chapters 2 and 3 to delineate the concepts of responsibility and responsible drinking, it is very clear that driving an automobile while having a BAC of .05 or above constitutes an irresponsible act. It is also true that driving an automobile while having a BAC of .10, .15, or higher constitutes a more irresponsible act than driving while having a BAC of .05. Many states in fact have laws which attempt to take into account a driver's level of intoxication in order to assess a fair and appropriate penalty for this form of irresponsible behavior. These matters are also a reflection of the concept of gradients of responsibility which was discussed in earlier chapters.

Most people have little difficulty accepting the fact that it is irresponsible to drive while intoxicated. However, people tend to disagree about the definition of "intoxication." In my clinical experience, very few people who are arrested for DUI or DWI and have BAC's within the range of .05 to .12 believe that they were intoxicated or "under the influence" of alcohol when they were arrested. They did not perceive themselves as inebriated when they were driving or at the time of arrest. Yet, the legal fact is that they were driving while intoxicated. Many of these individuals perceive themselves as under the influence or drunk only when they are relatively incoherent, have grossly impaired gait and slurred speech, and are perhaps physically ill as a result of drinking. They simply do not understand how little ethanol ingestion is required to produce a legally defined level of impairment or intoxication.

In fact, it is understandable how many people leave a party or social function after having consumed four or five alcoholic beverages and then are arrested for drinking and driving. Many of these people do not realize that they are impaired. Some have been drinking and driving with some degree of regularity for years but had never previously been arrested for this offense. Tragically, about 5 percent of our drivers are habitual DUI offenders. I recently treated a Colorado man who had a history of twenty-eight DUI convictions and nineteen driving without a license convictions in Colorado during a four-year period. He continued to drink and drive and had only spent a total of thirty days in jail for all of these convictions! Yet, the most basic reality in all of these situations is that driving with a BAC of .05 or over is irresponsible. This behavior is irresponsible regardless of circumstances and regardless of the driver's actual BAC.

While it is at least relatively easy for most people to understand and accept that it is irresponsible to operate an automobile or other vehicle while having a BAC of .05 or higher, the issue of driving with a BAC *under* .05 is more confusing. Is it responsible for a person to drive a vehicle if he or she has a BAC of .04 or .02? More fundamentally, is it responsible for a person to drive after any imbibing, regardless of blood alcohol concentration?

Obviously, according to the legal definition and legal parameters of drinking and driving it is *responsible* to drive if one has any BAC level under .05. Yet, as indicated earlier in this chapter, a BAC of only .05 results in several areas of driver impairment. Very low level BAC concentrations (.02–.04) may significantly impair the driving skills and abilities of many and perhaps all drivers. People who drink very little are especially affected by ethanol. Individuals who have not eaten in several hours or people who are stressed, emotionally disturbed, physically ill, or taking other mood-altering drugs may manifest significant driving impairments after consuming only two or three alcoholic beverages.

In view of these realities, the only truly responsible solution to the question of BAC level and driving safety is simply not driving after *any* drinking. It is irresponsible to drink and drive regardless of the driver's BAC level! Think about this position for a minute. Would an airline pilot be acting responsibly if he consumed only "two or three" cocktails while flying two or three hundred people from New York to Denver? The pilot's BAC in such a situation would not exceed .05. Perhaps another way to look at this situation would be to ask yourself if you would want to be a passenger on this airplane? How would you feel about your family dentist having a "couple" of drinks before working on your son or daughter's teeth? How about your surgeon having a martini or two before your coronary bypass operation or your "shrink" consuming a few beers during or before your next therapy session?

Driving demands our full attention and requires many skills, judgments, behaviors, and cognitions—just like flying or doing surgery. Pace and

Cross (1984) report that a driver might make approximately 100 decisions during every mile of highway driving and more than two hundred decisions per mile while driving in urban traffic. Clearly, it is irresponsible to drink and drive. It is irresponsible to drive after consuming two or three drinks just as it is irresponsible to drive after drinking ten alcoholic beverages.

It is also irresponsible for an individual to drive an automobile or operate any kind of vehicle after smoking marijuana, doing "coke," or ingesting any other kind of mood-altering drug. All of the illicit as well as legal or prescription mood-altering drugs impair driving performance. The vast majority of people would not want to fly with a pilot who "did a couple of joints" while flying or be operated on by a surgeon that "did a couple of lines" before beginning a surgical procedure.

Alcohol is a causative factor in over 50 percent of *all* accidental deaths—not just automobile deaths! In recent years we have experienced an increase in alcohol-related accidents involving all forms of transportation. Clearly, the most responsible solution to these problems rests with the old adage "if you drive, don't drink" or "if you drink, don't drive."

SUMMARY

American's have combined alcohol and driving for several decades. Historically, we have been a "one for the road" society. People who grew up in the 1940s through the 1960s seem to have been largely unaware of the various risks that are associated with drinking and driving. However, the general public has become far more aware of these realities over the past fifteen years, and the American tradition of drinking and operating cars and other vehicles is under increasing attack. Organizations such as Mothers Against Drunk Drivers (MADD), the National Council on Alcoholism (NCA) and the National Institute of Alcohol Abuse and Alcoholism (NIAAA) have played very significant roles in the process of educating Americans about the devastating realities of drinking and driving.

The consequences of drinking and driving were outlined in this chapter. Although the odds of being arrested for driving after drinking are roughly 1 in 2,000 (Timkin, 1986), the consequences of alcohol use in combination with driving are truly devastating. Approximately 25,000 people are killed each year on our highways by drinking drivers, nearly 500,000 people are injured each year on our highways by drinking drivers, and drunk driving is the leading single cause of death among young drivers. Alcohol is involved in over 50 percent of all accidental deaths!

Several of the physiological and psychomotor effects of alcohol ingestion were discussed in this chapter. According to the laws of most states, a driver is considered to be intoxicated when his or her blood alcohol concentration (BAC) is .10 or above. A BAC of .05 or above results in legal impairment. A drinker generally needs to consume three ounces of ethanol in a period of one-and-one-half to two hours to have a BAC of .05. It also takes about one hour for the human body to metabolize one ounce of 86 proof ethanol. The drinker's overall health, weight, and other factors may also influence an individual's pattern of consumption and different responses to imbibing. The minimal driving impairments that are associated with a BAC of only .05 were also listed in this chapter.

Finally, the responsible-irresponsible parameters of alcohol use in combination with driving were elucidated. Although the law defines any driving or use of a vehicle by a person with a BAC of less than .05 as responsible, I have suggested that any drinking while driving is clearly irresponsible. According to this position, it is irresponsible for a person with a BAC of .02 or .04 to operate an automobile or any other vehicle. It is also irresponsible for people to fly airplanes, drive boats and motorcycles, or operate snowmobiles and other machinery after *any* drinking.

It is important for alcohol and drug education and treatment personnel to educate the general public about the effects of alcohol use on driving and all other forms of human behavior! There are many irrational myths that need to be dispelled in the realm of drinking and driving. For example, drinking a cup or two of coffee after an evening of beer drinking will not "sober up" a person. Driving thirty or forty miles per hour on the freeway after consuming several alcoholic beverages is not a solution to the problem of driving while intoxicated. The only responsible solution to this problem is the one that has been phrased by hundreds of other health educators and behavior scientists: "If you drive don't drink, or if you do drink, for God's sake don't drive."

Chapter 9

ENTERTAINING AND SOCIALIZING: TO SERVE OR NOT TO SERVE?

THE AMERICAN WAY

Americans tend to be very social and gregarious people. We love to entertain and we thrive on a great deal of social interaction. Indeed, a hallmark of our traditional American way of life is that of gathering together for myriad social events and special purposes. Family reunions and "get-togethers," "block parties," joining a fraternity or sorority and fraternity and sorority "functions," before the game "tailgate parties," weddings and holidays, promotions and retirements, birthdays, and even funerals are but a few of the social events that millions of Americans participate in on a regular basis. We seem to have an uncanny ability to use any reason or "excuse" to get together for a party or social interaction!

The American way of entertaining and socializing also traditionally involves drinking and sometimes florid alcohol abuse. Many Americans seem to feel almost compelled to offer their neighbors or friends a beer or a cocktail when they drop by for a visit. We include alcohol in the vast majority of our social interactions and social rituals. Ethanol is the great American social lubricant. Americans drink at "happy hours," football and baseball games, on fishing trips and vacations, and with "business" lunches. Alcohol is an integral ingredient at wedding receptions, New Year's Eve parties, some funerals, and very often church activities. In sum, drinking is a major component in a diversity of American social activities. This reality also applies to the social interactions and processes of virtually every other culture and nation in the world.

The human species has long utilized ethanol as a social lubricant. Alcohol serves a diversity of social purposes. Government officials and heads of state may feel more comfortable with each other after consuming a few drinks. Alcohol has been used for centuries to facilitate courtship, romance, and sexual interactions. Alcohol has also been utilized to accentuate human religious and festive experiences for thousands of years.

When we begin to consider the historic realities of alcohol use in connection with human social interaction it is certainly not surprising that modern Americans involve alcohol in virtually all of their entertaining and socializing activities. However, in recent years people have begun to question the "standard procedure" of serving unlimited or even limited numbers of alcoholic beverages to their guests. More people seem to be desirous of entertaining and socializing without drinking, and surely fewer people feel obligated to provide alcoholic beverages at parties and social functions. Most people do not want to feel as though they *must* drink or serve alcoholic beverages in order to be "social" or to be a "good host."

TO SERVE OR NOT TO SERVE: RESPONSIBILITY ISSUES

The decision to serve or not serve alcoholic beverages at a party or social activity can be very important for the host as well as his or her guests. This is a matter of choice. Whenever a person is entertaining or has some form of social get-together he or she must choose to serve alcoholic drinks or not serve alcoholic drinks. Furthermore, guests at a social function choose to imbibe, not to imbibe, or how much to drink if the host in fact provides alcoholic beverages at the party or function.

For several decades, if not longer, most Americans have entertained their friends and neighbors by serving them cocktails and various alcoholic beverages. It is reasonable to hypothesize that the vast majority of people who have historically entertained their guests with alcoholic drinks have not been particularly concerned about the responsible-irresponsible dimensions of this pattern of social behavior. However, in recent years many people have become increasingly aware of the potential liability risks that are specifically associated with the practice of serving alcoholic drinks to guests. No doubt this increased awareness about the liability risks of giving guests who attend a private party or social get-together alcoholic beverages stems from lawsuits and legal actions that were first initiated against bars and owners of various establishments that sell alcoholic beverages. These suits and legal actions have received a good deal of media attention over the past ten years. More recently, such legal actions have involved not only bartenders and the owners of establishments that sell alcohol but also people who simply serve alcoholic beverages to other people at parties and social functions in their homes. These cases have facilitated a growing awareness upon the part of people in general that simply serving drinks to friends, neighbors, or colleagues within the privacy of one's home can indeed be a very risky business!

These issues have confronted Americans with the fact that it can be irresponsible to serve alcoholic beverages to people at parties and social outings. There are a number of factors that operate to determine the responsible-irresponsible dimensions of serving alcoholic drinks to guests in various social situations. Foremost, it is clearly irresponsible for a host to continue serving alcoholic beverages to a guest who is intoxicated. Such a situation closely parallels that of a bartender or employee in a liquor store selling alcohol to an intoxicated customer. If a bartender continues to serve alcoholic beverages to an inebriated patron and the patron subsequently leaves the bar and injures himself or someone else, the *server* may be legally liable and responsible for the resulting injuries. Likewise, a host who serves alcoholic drinks to intoxicated guests at his or her home may be held legally responsible if the guest injures himself or others after leaving the host's home.

These situations become more complex and legally confusing when the host is not knowingly serving alcoholic drinks to a guest who is intoxicated. Can a host or bartender be held responsible in situations where he or she serves a guest or patron only one or two alcoholic beverages? Can a host be expected to know when a guest has "had too much" or is legally impaired? What about the guest who "sneaks" drinks from the host's bar *after* the host has refused to serve him more drinks? How about the host who teasingly entices a problem drinker or alcoholic to have "a drink or two" at his or her party? Who is responsible if the problem drinker in this situation goes on a "binge" a week later and subsequently kills someone in an automobile accident while driving under the influence?

There are no simple or "easy" legal answers to questions such as these. Each year thousands of these types of cases do require litigation to resolve. As noted earlier in the chapter, the guest or patron in all of these situations must share responsibility with the host, bartender, or owner of the establishment which sells and/or distributes alcoholic beverages. After all, the guest does choose to drink or not drink the beverages which his or her guest chooses to serve! The patron actually pays money to be served alcoholic drinks, and thus he or she actually owns an alcoholic beverage once it is paid for. After buying a drink, the patron must decide what to do with it; he or she is responsible for the decision to ingest the drink.

Perhaps a general solution to several of these questions would be to hold the server and drinker equally responsible in all liability situations when the drinker has a BAC of .05 or above. Hosts or bartenders and sales clerks at liquor stores could ask or require that guests and customers take an alcohol breathalizer test before leaving a party, leaving a bar, or purchasing liquor. A host or bartender might even require a guest or partner to take this test *prior* to being served an alcoholic drink.

Another obvious solution to these situations would be for hosts to simply not serve alcoholic beverages to their guests. In fact, increasing numbers of people are choosing not to serve alcoholic beverages at their parties or they are consciously deciding to limit the number of drinks they serve to guests. Hosts who choose not to serve alcoholic beverages to their guests are not confronted with the various responsibility and liability risks and issues that have been discussed. It is responsible as well as socially acceptable and appropriate for hosts to choose to omit alcohol from their parties and entertaining activities! It is also nice not to have to worry about "how" or "if" guests will make it home safely from your party.

An obvious solution to the issue of entertaining and socializing with alcohol is for the host to always serve responsibly. While some people might argue that it is categorically irresponsible or even evil to serve alcoholic beverages to anyone under any circumstance, most believe that a host or hostess can serve alcoholic beverages responsibly. However, people can be expected to argue about the parameters of responsible hosting with alcoholic beverages. It is also logical to expect that many people simply are not cognizant of the basic parameters of responsible drinking or socializing with ethanol.

No doubt, most hosts who serve their guests alcoholic drinks would resist or reject the idea of administering alcohol breathalizer tests to their guests in order to demonstrate that they are serving alcohol responsibly! The pragmatic aspects of requiring guests or customers to routinely take a breathalizer test in order to be given alcoholic drinks or purchase alcohol can place a number of unrealistic demands on all people involved in these situations. Thus, it is important for hosts and hostesses to understand the fundamental principals of entertaining and socializing with alcohol in a responsible manner.

RESPONSIBLE ENTERTAINING AND SOCIALIZING WITH ALCOHOL

If you choose to serve your guests alcoholic drinks, it is absolutely imperative that you do so responsibly! Regardless of the social situation or nature of a social get-together, the host and hostess who provide their guests with alcoholic beverages are largely responsible for the various consequences of alcohol use in these social environments. The following guidelines are suggested as measures that you can take in order to assure that you are serving alcoholic drinks responsibly:

(1) Never serve alcoholic drinks to minors.
(2) Never serve alcoholic drinks to friends or people you know or have reason to believe are alcohol abusers, alcoholics, or other drug abusers.
(3) Always limit the number of drinks you serve to individuals at a party or social function. I recommend that you attempt to limit the number of drinks to one per person every 1½ to 2 hours.
(4) Always serve non-alcoholic drinks at parties and actively display these beverages and actively reinforce non-alcoholic drinking—encourage guests to drink soda, coffee, tea, and other non-alcoholic beverages.
(5) Serve a variety of foods, snacks, and preferably high-protein foods at parties and social get-togethers.
(6) Consider serving low-alcohol content beverages: the "light" beers and wines rather than whiskey, vodka, or bourbon.
(7) Stop serving alcoholic beverages an hour or two before the party ends.
(8) Mingle with your guests; observe their consumption patterns and behaviors, and instruct those who actually serve the drinks and mixed drinks (bartenders and other hosts/hostesses) to do the same.
(9) Don't hesitate to "cut off" guests who are becoming intoxicated or behaving inappropriately.
(10) *Never* allow a guest to leave your party and then drive home impaired or intoxicated.

These general guidelines can be applied to virtually all social situations that might involve serving alcohol. For example consider a New Year's Eve party or a birthday party that you might host. It is just as illegal and irresponsible to serve a minor alcoholic beverages at a New Year's Eve party as it is on any other day or evening of the year! It is categorically irresponsible to serve an alcoholic ethanol anytime under any social circumstances.

It can be difficult to limit or monitor the actual number of drinks that are served to guests at a party. Obviously, the more guests the greater the difficulty in monitoring numbers of drinks and drinking behaviors. However, it is relatively easy to serve non-alcoholic drinks, foods, and low-alcohol content beverages at parties. The host or hostess can also decide when to stop serving alcoholic beverages to guests. Hosts need to realize that it is okay to refuse to serve alcoholic drinks to intoxicated guests. Indeed, the host and hostess need to bear in mind that they are at least partially responsible for the various alcohol-related behaviors of their guests.

One simple strategy that can be utilized in order to limit the number of drinks guests consume at a social function is to limit the amount or quantity of alcohol that the host makes available to guests. For example, a hostess might invite eight or ten people to a dinner party but only have one or two quarts of wine available for her guests. The host who invites three or four friends over to watch a Sunday afternoon football game might have one or two six-packs of beer available for his guests. In similar situations when a limited number of "mixed drinks" are offered to guests it may also be helpful for the host to use a shot glass in order to carefully measure and monitor the exact amount of ethanol that he is serving guests.

Finally, it can be difficult for many hosts and hostesses to muster up enough courage to be assertive with impaired guests and either "cut them off" or insist that they not drive home after the social function. Hostesses and hosts need to periodically remind themselves that they are in charge of their party and they are also entitled to say no to alcohol for an intoxicated or impaired guest. When it comes to the issue of intoxicated guests leaving the party, it is the host's responsibility to (1) offer to drive the guest home, (2) arrange for another guest or someone else to take the impaired guest home, (3) call a taxi for the impaired guest, (4) offer to have the guest spend the night, (5) possibly restrain the guest and/or take the guest's car keys, or (6) actually call the police to detain the guest or provide the guest with ample reinforcement not to operate his or her vehicle while under the influence of alcohol.

The host and/or hostesses are responsible for actively initiating and carrying out these alternatives for intoxicated guests. With firmness, tact, and positive encouragement it is usually possible to get even a belligerent guest to accept a ride home or perhaps remain at the host's home for the night. In extreme situations, it may be necessary to summon the police. In these cases, the police are usually very courteous, understanding, and they may actually take the guest to his or her residence. The best solution to all of these potential crisis situations is to eliminate them *before* they develop, by refusing in all ways to allow guests to drink to the point of impairment or intoxication.

Guests do not measure the success or failure of a party according to the severity of their "hangover" the morning after! A good host or hostess is also interested in the total well-being of his or her guests. Good hosts do not want their guests to be sick the next day, and they certainly do not want their guests to be arrested on the way home or killed in an automobile accident. Both guests and hosts want to be able to remember what they did and said during the course of a party! Thus, hosts and guests both benefit in myriad ways when alcohol is served responsibly at parties and social functions.

It is also important for hosts and hostesses to remember that they are role models at parties and social get-togethers. When hosts drink nonalcoholic beverages, eat snacks, or sip one or two alcoholic drinks during the course of a party they in effect model responsible alcohol use/nonuse social behaviors for their guests. In this respect, hosts and hostesses set the pace or style of alcohol use at their parties. Hosts who drink heavily, "push drinks" on guests, or in other ways encourage irresponsible drinking upon the part of their guests are behaving irresponsibly!

Again, the reader needs to bear in mind that the guidelines presented in this chapter apply to virtually all entertaining and socializing situations. Weddings and receptions, birthdays, family reunions, office parties, holiday get-togethers, and parties with friends and neighbors are all social situations where these basic guidelines for responsible alcohol use can be applied.

Several months ago a colleague's secretary told me that she was having a difficult time deciding whether or not to buy her soon-to-be-sixteen-year-old daughter "her own" bottle of champagne with which to celebrate her sixteenth birthday. Another neighborhood acquaintance shared with my wife that she and her husband were going to buy three 16-gallon kegs of beer for their son and his friends in order "to celebrate" their son's graduation from high school. In both of these situations, the parent's seemed to be asking for our advice on these matters; perhaps they were asking for our "permission" to provide their children and friends with alcoholic beverages? According to the guidelines presented in this chapter, it would be grossly irresponsible and inappropriate for the parents in these specific situations to have provided their *children* with alcoholic beverages for the purposes of celebrating a birthday or high school graduation.

When in doubt about responsible socializing and entertaining with alcohol it may be helpful for you to take a few minutes and reread or consult this chapter!

SUMMARY

Americans have a long tradition of socializing and entertaining with alcohol. Indeed, ethanol is the great American social lubricant. Alcohol is often an integral component of our family reunions, birthday parties, New Year's Eve parties, "block parties," fraternity initiations, and various other social activities. All too often, we also tend to abuse alcohol and serve alcohol irresponsibly in these various social contexts.

The recondite as well as practical aspects of socializing and entertaining with alcohol were discussed in this chapter. The legal, moral, and ethical dimensions of serving guests alcoholic drinks were outlined. Hosts and hostesses as well as liquor store owners and bartenders tend to be concerned about the legal consequences of giving guests drinks or selling and serving alcoholic beverages to patrons. It is reasonable to assume that alcohol breathalizer tests will be used more frequently in the future to help liquor store owners and bartenders and perhaps even hosts determine whether or not to serve or sell alcoholic beverages.

It is certainly easy, appropriate, and responsible for hosts and hostesses to choose to omit alcohol from their parties and social activities. However, when hostesses or hosts choose to serve alcohol at their social get-togethers it is imperative that they serve responsibly. Ten specific guidelines for responsible hosting with ethanol are provided in this chapter. Briefly, it is important for the hosts to (1) limit the amount/number of drinks served at a party, (2) observe and supervise the drinking behaviors of guests, (3) actively encourage the consumption of non-alcoholic beverages, (4) serve a variety of foods and snacks at social functions, (5) serve low-alcohol content drinks, (6) stop serving drinks one-and-one-half to two hours before the party ends, (7) refuse to serve guests who are beginning to become inebriated, and (8) never permit a guest to leave a party intoxicated.

These guidelines can be applied to virtually all parties and social functions that involve alcohol. Specific guidelines were also delineated for effectively dealing with guests who might become impaired at a party. These individuals might need to be taken home by the host or perhaps even encouraged to spend the night at the host's home. With firmness, tact, and positive encouragement it is usually possible for hosts and hostesses to serve or even refuse to serve alcoholic beverages to guests in a responsible manner. The success or failure of a party is not measured via the number of guests who are sick, have hangovers or suffering from amnesia or blackouts the day after! Clearly, hosts and guests are both benefited in myriad ways when alcohol is served and ingested responsibly at social functions.

Chapter 10

RESPONSIBLE DRINKING IN THE BUSINESS WORLD

KEEPING THE BUSINESS MACHINE WELL-OILED

America is a huge business machine. All of us are somehow components of the American business machine. Some people work on assembly lines, while others are managers, supervisors, or engineers. Every person in the business world is a part in this machine. Regardless of occupation, age, sex, or social class, we are parts of this business machine even in death. Our loved ones and survivors in death must pick out a casket, grave site, consider cremation, and always transact the business of death and dying by paying the final bill!

The American business machine also has a long tradition of being well-oiled and infused with oil, that is, alcohol—our all-purpose social and business lubricant is the "oil" of the business world. Many people believe that alcohol literally makes and keeps our business world running. The "two or three" martini business lunch has been a bona fide tax deduction for years! Business has been "conducted" over a "few drinks" in this country and throughout the world for hundreds if not thousands of years. Contracts are signed, business transactions are initiated and designed, and money is made or lost via drinks and dinner or lunch.

Promotions and successes or failures within the business world may also be determined in part by alcohol and one's alcohol use behaviors. When I was a young first lieutenant in the army we were told that it was important to belong to the officer's club and attend certain "happy hours" and social functions *if* we wanted to be promoted or be career officers. Middle- and upper-level management personnel in most, if not all, corporations and industries have been confronted with similar social realities. Indeed, people at all levels of the business world learn that it may be politically beneficial as well as efficacious from the standpoint of career development and career advancement to imbibe with peers and/or supervisors.

The business world has also maintained a long history of drinking norms or social rules and regulations that govern patterns of alcohol use in these environments. For example, Marines are expected to be "macho drinkers" and drinking serves many social and interpersonal functions within the military environment. Yet, after a night of heavy drinking and perhaps acute intoxication a Marine is expected to be able to "stand tall" and "soldier" at 5:30 A.M.! By the same token, an executive vice-president of General Motors Corporation may be overtly or tacitly expected to have a "few drinks" with colleagues over dinner, but any observable indication of intoxication is unacceptable and frowned upon by peers and superiors.

Perhaps the basic belief system about alcohol use in the business world has long been "drink, but for God's sake don't get drunk." This belief system and code of social behavior also encompasses the idea that *intoxication* should be denied, secretive, and must not occur within the context of "business." Thus, it is socially acceptable to conduct business while drinking and even when intoxicated as long as one does not *appear* to be drunk or intoxicated in these situations. The belief system that supports this behavior is "drink, but for God's sake don't *appear* to be drunk."

It is also important to point out that any alcohol use may be frowned upon in some business and corporate settings. Indeed, corporate managers and the business world in general are becoming progressively more cognizant of the various risks and costs that are associated with alcohol use in the world of work.

THE PRICE WE PAY

All of us pay the price for alcohol abuse and alcoholism. We certainly pay the price for alcohol misuse in the business world! And in reality there are a diversity of *prices* to be paid as a result of alcohol abuse in the world of work. Bear in mind that all of us share the cost of alcohol misuse in the business world, not just the drinker and his or her family, or "the" corporation, business, and employers. Consider these facts: (1) alcoholism and alcohol abuse cost industry (all of us!) between $40 and $50 billion per year; (2) Americans spend approximately $250 billion a year on health care; and (3) about half of our annual health care cost ($125 *billion*) is paid by employers in the form of employee health benefits (Wallace, 1985). Furthermore, it is estimated that about 10 percent of the work force is alcoholic or alcohol-drug impaired.

Irresponsible drinking and alcohol use in the world of work affect health care costs. The costs of problem drinking in industry and the business world are measured in terms of job absenteeism or lost time, alcohol-related illnesses and accidents, staff turnover, disability benefits, reduced worker productivity, lower quality of workmanship, poor judgment and poor decision making at all levels of industry, lawsuits and legal involvements, and conflictual employee-employer-management relations. In some work settings, it is rather commonplace for employees to drink, smoke marijuana, or use other drugs over the lunch break or while working. No doubt, the common hangover costs industry hundreds of thousands of dollars a year! The simple fact is that thousands of Americans drink and ingest other mood-altering chemicals before, during, and after work. They also engage in these costly behaviors on an everyday basis and all of us end up paying the price.

Wallace (1985) reports that in 1980 the estimated cost of alcoholism and problem drinking to the state of California was $4.28 billion. About 1.5 million alcoholics and problem drinkers from the state's populace of 24 million people caused this tremendous expense. Chemical dependency problems in Minnesota cost the state between $1 and $2 billion annually. In Georgia the estimated annual cost of alcohol abuse in business and industry was $350 million in 1981. This state paid an additional $217 million in hospital health care, and $13 million for law enforcement and criminal justice as a result of alcohol misuse in 1981. During the same year, Alabama businesses and industry spent nearly $500 million for alcohol abuse, and New York businesses paid over $1 billion as a result of alcohol abuse.

These costly realities have caused many corporations and businesses to develop programs that are designed to (1) help troubled employees and (2) reduce the costs of alcohol and drug abuse to industry and the business world. These programs are referred to as *EAPs*, or employee assistance programs. They have consistently demonstrated that corporations and businesses can save millions of dollars by identifying and treating alcohol-drug impaired workers. For example, one study conducted at Oldsmobile's Lansing, Michigan plant demonstrated that alcoholic employees who received treatment for their alcoholism were able to reduce their lost man-hours by 52 percent following treatment! The employees who received treatment in this study saved their employer's $233,000 in just one year. Kennecott Copper Company was able to reduce its absenteeism by over 50 percent by instituting a program that helped alcohol-abusing employees enter treatment. At General Motors, approximately 42,000 workers or 7 percent of the GM work force were involved in the company's EAP program. It is significant that over 25,000 of these workers had alcohol problems (Wallace, 1985). Involvement in GM's EAP program reduced time off the job by 40 percent, and health and accident benefit payments were reduced by 60 percent!

Industrial research clearly demonstrates time and again that it is significantly less expensive to treat alcoholic employees than it is to recruit, train, and employ new personnel. Furthermore, industrial EAP programs often report 80–90 percent success rates. Most employees can be successfully rehabilitated, and these employees generally save their companies about $1,000 per year (per employee) in sickness and accident disability benefit payments.

The message from all this is really quite clear: alcohol and the business world do not mix! Unfortunately, many Americans are convinced that alcohol runs the business world. These individuals believe that alcohol is somehow an integral component of effective business interactions. In reality, the alcohol-business world mix is a costly, inefficient, and highly flammable mix. Our business world suffers from an annual multi-billion dollar hangover, and sadly, we are all paying the price for this malaise.

GUIDELINES FOR RESPONSIBLE ALCOHOL USE IN THE BUSINESS WORLD

Realizing that our American heritage includes mixing alcohol with business and at the same time understanding the diversity of irrational and costly aspects of this tradition presents a very conflictual dilemma. Once again we are confronted with the question of responsible alcohol use in another global situation or context: the world of work. Is there such a "thing" as responsible alcohol use in the business world? And if there is, what are the guidelines for responsible drinking in the business world? While there are once again no easy or simple answers to these questions, there are a number of general guidelines for responsible alcohol use in the world of work.

The following guidelines for responsible alcohol use in the business world are presented with one major caveat in mind: *any* alcohol use in the world of work may be irresponsible, and any irresponsible alcohol use in the business world can be and often is disastrous!

(1) It is probably in your best interest and your employee's best interest for you to *never* mix alcohol and business.
(2) If you do choose to drink and conduct business simultaneously, never consume more than one or two ounces of ethanol during the course of *any* business transaction, whether it takes one hour or six hours to transact the actual business. Quantity of alcohol consumed is important, and any alcohol use may affect business judgment and reasoning.
(3) The shorter and more important the business transaction, the more important it is for you to abstain or limit your drinking.
(4) Never make it a consistent habit to mix even one or two drinks with your business involvements.
(5) Don't allow your business colleagues to influence your decisions about alcohol use in the context of work.
(6) Remember that "free drinks" are not the key to good business or a "solid deal"—it can be easier for some people to choose to drink alcoholic beverages if "the company" or another person in a business situation is literally "buying the drinks," and
(7) Always keep in mind the fact that even one or two drinks can affect your ability to make timely, rational, and lucid business decisions.

Drinking with a business colleague or boss is never a job requirement. Furthermore, imbibing with others in the business world is no predictor of business acumen or success. However, a drink in some business situations may be appropriate and relaxing.

The ceremonial chemistry of alcohol and business can be floridly irrational. Having several drinks with your realtor at the time of "closing" on your new home, or getting "smashed" with office colleagues when you get that long-awaited-for promotion, or "unwinding" every Friday afternoon at "happy hour" with the office staff can be "risky business." Americans consistently associate drinking with these small or minor celebrations and social rituals.

Many large corporations have traditions of providing alcoholic beverages for employees at company "functions." Having been a consultant for several large corporate groups, I am personally all too familiar with the negative consequences that can be associated with these "corporate social functions." The barbeques and keg parties that one major corporation sponsored for several years here in Colorado Springs consistently resulted in alcohol-facilitated marital fights, car wrecks, assaults and fights between employees, and a lot of broken homes and medical expenses. These functions involved hundreds of employees and their families and they were scheduled on a regular basis several times each year!

The military also has a long tradition of rewarding troops with alcohol. Whenever the unit passes a difficult inspection, everyone is rewarded with "free beer" at the NCO club. Military "hail and farewell" parties as well as promotion parties are notorious drinking situations.

In all of these business situations it can be very easy for many people to break some or all of the guidelines for responsible alcohol use. Many factors are associated with this reality. A simple but important factor is numbers. For example, if a company sponsors a cookout or Christmas party for several hundred employees, how can any individual or even group of individuals be expected to monitor the drinking behaviors of the group? As noted in earlier chapters, it can be difficult to monitor or control the drinking behaviors of very small groups and even loved ones. Furthermore, it is always somewhat difficult to stop or "cut off" the alcohol use of anyone under any set of circumstances!

Corporations, management, and individual employers are also beginning to realize the liability issues and risks that are associated with alcohol use in the world of work. If General Motors, Digital, or similar large corporations choose to provide alcoholic beverages for their employees at company parties or "functions" they (meaning the corporation or employer) are at least partially responsible for any injury or destructive consequences that might be associated with an employee's use of alcohol in such a context. These liability risks are extended to situations where managers and supervisors drink with each other or employees, any alcohol use in the actual work environment, or corporate policy supporting and reinforcing alcohol use in connection with work or company social functions.

All of these realities are associated with the first guideline for responsible alcohol use in the business world! It is simply responsible and prudent for any worker, employer, or company to choose not to mix alcohol and business in any amount or under any circumstances! Thus, it is appropriate and socially adroit to choose not to drink within the world of business.

Beyond the alternative of not drinking in the context of business, it is prudent for businessmen who do drink while conducting business to strictly limit their consumption. Thus, an occasional drink by non-alcoholic or non-alcohol-abusing businessmen or businesswomen may not be problematic. It is important to avoid the "trap" of consistently using alcohol as a business "crutch" or lubricant, and, indeed, any consistent use of alcohol in the context of work or business is risky. Individuals at every level in the corporate ladder need to be assertive and think for themselves when it comes to the matters of alcohol use and drinking in the work environment. Don't acquiesce to peer or supervisor pressure to drink while conducting business. Free drinks, happy hours, and the company TGIF (Thank God It's Friday) club are poor excuses for mixing alcohol and work. Furthermore, free drinks, happy hours, and business interactions that are literally "soaked" in alcohol are not the keys to business success and job promotions. Everyone in the business world needs to remember one very basic and simple fact: "a couple" of drinks *can* impair judgment and thus negatively affect job performance and generalized business acumen.

Finally, corporate morality always includes the issue of responsible alcohol use. Individual employers, supervisors, and corporate heads as well as all workers in any corporate structure need to be cognizant of the various complex issues that are associated with alcohol use in the world of work.

Most large corporations and all government agencies have developed employee assistance programs (EAP) over the past several years. As indicated earlier, these programs are developed to assist and provide treatment for employees with alcohol and drug problems. Unfortunately, EAP programs in part represent industry's attempt to counteract irresponsible or "enabling" alcohol use policies that have been operational for decades.

EVALUATING ALCOHOL USE IN THE WORLD OF WORK

It may be periodically helpful for the reader to evaluate his or her alcohol use as well as the drinking behaviors of others within the specific context of work and business. The evaluation of alcohol use and drinking behaviors in the work environment can be accomplished by focusing upon the following areas: (1) Frequency of drinking or alcohol use in combination with work and within the work environment; (2) number or percentage of people drinking in the work milieu; (3) objective comparison of individual and group patterns of alcohol use in the business realm (How many drinks do I consume in a given business-alcohol use transaction or how many drinks do colleagues consume in these situations?);

and (4) assessing if it is necessary, appropriate, or required that alcohol use be a component of any business transaction or work environment.

By focusing clearly upon these aspects of drinking within the business environment the reader will be able to better evaluate or assess the use-abuse, appropriateness, and rational-irrational social dimensions of his or others' work-related patterns of alcohol use.

Drinking in the business world is clearly pathologic and problematic when an individual begins to (1) experience job performance problems as a result of alcohol and/or drug use, (2) arrive late for work or leave early as a result of drinking, (3) miss work due to drinking, especially Mondays and/or Fridays, (4) experience significant conflicts with supervisors and/or colleagues as a result of drinking. Quite simply, an individual has a drinking problem whenever his or her drinking causes any type of problem in the work environment. The "troubled employee" frequently "calls in sick," forgets important deadlines, makes more and more on-the-job errors, is angry, defensive, irritable, and conflicted in relationships with fellow workers, and progressively becomes more irresponsible in all areas of job functioning. These key signs or symptoms of the "troubled employee" are usually caused by alcoholism or excessive alcohol use.

Whenever a person begins to exhibit these behaviors in the work environment it is only rational to suspect that alcohol and/or other drug abuse is the primary source of conflict. If an employee or employer is experiencing a drinking problem which is affecting his or her job performance and general work behaviors, this person should be actively encouraged to enter a rehabilitation program or some appropriate form of professional treatment. The key to success in these situations is early identification and early intervention. Many industrial problems can be prevented by early intervention—the process of helping conflicted employees before they actually become "troubled employees" in the sense of actually getting into trouble!

Employers and corporations are developing more effective EAPs and encouraging more and more people to seek assistance before their drinking and emotional problems become truly out of control within the business world. These programs teach people to ask for help or seek out help before problems become out of control. Within the business world, thousands of counselors and employee assistance workers are actively developing programs and alternatives to alcohol and drug use.

All people need to clearly understand the hazards and potential dangers of mixing alcohol and business. Furthermore, we need to consciously understand the irrational socialization and brainwashing that takes place relative to the issues of alcohol use in the world of work. As a boss or employee, you do not "owe it to yourself" to have a few drinks with lunch or after work because your job is so demanding, frustrating, or whatever else. Most of the logic that supports alcohol/drug use in the business world is clearly irrational and self-defeating. Indeed, more people are concerned about alcohol misuse in the world of work simply because more people are becoming aware of the irrational behaviors and "stinkin' thinkin' " that occurs when alcohol is combined with work and business.

SUMMARY

The American business machine has been "well oiled" for several decades. Indeed, American's have a long tradition of mixing alcohol and business. While we expect to drink and work or conduct business, we frown upon overt or acute intoxication in the work place.

The price that all Americans pay for alcohol misuse in the world of work is tremendous. Approximately 10 percent of our work force is alcohol-dependent, and drinkers in the work force cost all of us some $40 to $50 billion each year. The various costs of alcohol abuse in business as well as the cost benefits of employee assistance programs were explored in this chapter. Impaired employees can often be successfully rehabilitated, and treatment programs in industry are cost-effective.

Seven guidelines for responsible alcohol use in the business world were presented in this chapter. However, the reader needs to realize that *any* alcohol use in the world of work may result in irresponsible behaviors and poor business decision making. Whenever businessmen or businesswomen choose to imbibe within the context of business lunches, happy hours, company parties and social functions, or office meetings, they need to limit their consumption. Free drinks or a company policy that reinforces alcohol use are poor reasons or excuses for mixing alcohol and business.

Corporations, employers and supervisors, or workers who reinforce abusive patterns of alcohol consumption within the world of work are irresponsible and even liable. It is responsible and prudent for any corporation, employer, or worker to choose not to mix alcohol and/or other drugs in *any* amount in any business context.

The evaluation of drinking behaviors within the business world involves focusing upon (1) frequency and amount of consumption, (2) numbers and percentages of drinkers, (3) objective studies of drinking patterns and behaviors, and (4) the social, political, and psychological dimensions of alcohol use. Several of the characteristics of alcohol-impaired employees were also listed in this chapter. Declining job performance, missing work or frequent illness, and conflicts with coworkers or supervisors are often the "telltale" symptoms of problematic alcohol use in the world of work.

The bottom-line fact is simply that alcohol and business do not mix. Furthermore, the logic that supports alcohol/drug use in the business world is generally irrational and self-defeating. We are all better business persons when we are not under the influence!

Chapter 11

ALCOHOL AND SEX: IS THERE A RESPONSIBLE "MIX"?

THE LOVE POTION

In view of the fact that human beings have long relied upon ethanol as a social lubricant, it should not be particularly surprising that we also have a long history of using alcohol as a sexual lubricant. Indeed, we have probably tried every possible combination or concoction of alcohol and sex. Most people who "mix" alcohol and sex probably do so in order to somehow express their sexual feelings, impulses, and desires. These individuals simply use alcohol to be romantic or sexual. As a sexual lubricant, alcohol has been used to enhance and facilitate various sexual behaviors.

When alcohol enhances or seems to facilitate the expression of sexuality, it takes on the properties of a magical elixir or love potion. Sadly, for countless numbers of people alcohol appears to act as a love potion. These individuals learn to express their sexuality vis-à-vis ethanol, and they emotionally depend upon alcohol in order to be sexual. Tragically, alcohol becomes akin to a love potion for such people. Many of these individuals cannot be sexual or express their sexual needs and feelings in the absence of drinking. They become psychologically dependent upon alcohol and/or other drugs in order to be sexual and to express their sexual desires.

It is significant that alcohol and virtually all other mood-altering chemicals have been used for various sexual purposes. In general, however, human beings seem to use these agents to enhance their sexual responding. When people somehow believe that alcohol enhances their sexual responding they set themselves up to not only perceive ethanol as a magical "love potion" but also this particular learning set no doubt simply makes it easier for some to develop addiction problems.

In fact, alcohol is not a love potion. Alcohol is also not an aphrodisiac or a sexual elixir. Ethanol does change our perceptions and cognitions, and thus it may be easier for many people to *believe* that they are better or more sensual lovers after imbibing. Unfortunately, alcohol misuse is often a precursor to self-deception in the realm of sexuality and sexual functioning. What are the *real* relationships between alcohol use and sexual functioning?

ALCOHOL USE AND SEXUAL RESPONDING: A TOUCH OF REALITY

Many years ago, Shakespeare said of alcohol: "It provokes the desire, but it takes away the performance." This single statement is incredibly descript. Alcohol abuse and alcoholism (Forrest, 1983) can cause and/or contribute to all forms of sexual dysfunction. Even small amounts of ethanol can impair sexual responding. Thus, drinking can be a key contributing factor in cases of male impotence, retarded ejaculation, low sexual desire and arousal problems, frigidity or anorgasmia, and painful coitus. Research indicates that alcohol generally diminishes penile size, duration of erection, vaginal lubrication, vaginal pressure pulse, and other indicators of physiological sexual arousal.

The recent sexual research efforts of Masters and Johnson, Kolodney, Kaplan, Hartman and Fithian, and the LoPiccolo's clearly and consistently demonstrate that alcohol misuse is a frequent cause of various sexual dysfunctions and problems. Furthermore, heavy drinking and alcoholism are frequently associated with many forms of deviant sexual responding. For example, between 50 and 80 percent of cases of incest involve alcoholic and/or intoxicated fathers or step-fathers. Child molestation cases often involve alcohol. Nearly 50 percent of rapes are committed by males who have been drinking. Many homosexual acts as well as cases of exhibitionism are alcohol-facilitated.

It is very apparent that alcohol misuse can cause or facilitate a diversity of human sexual problems. Many of these sexual problems are truly devastating. Just a few weeks ago a young man consulted me about his depression and periodic acute alcohol abuse. Shortly after our therapy session began he became very upset as he shared with me how he periodically engaged in homosexual behavior following or in combination with heavy drinking. Tragically, he had also just learned from his physician that he had AIDS! He was afraid of dying and confused about his *inability* to engage in homosexual behavior in the absence of drinking and acute intoxication.

Most people do not understand that even small doses or amounts of ethanol can affect sexual responding. Many seem to believe that a person must consume large quantities of alcohol in order to develop a sexual dysfunction or engage in sexually deviant behavior. Such is not the case. Some males experience ejaculatory problems after consuming only two or three alcoholic beverages. Often, men and women act out sexually after consuming small amounts of alcohol and/or other mood-altering chemicals.

In spite of these realities, many, if not most, men and women *believe* that they are better lovers after imbibing. As touched upon earlier, many people feel more sexually aroused and believe that they are better lovers after drinking. Research indicates that these self-sexual perceptions are generally fallacious and distorted. A study by Wilson and Lawson (1976) reported a negative linear relationship between increasing levels of alcohol consumption and physiological measures of sexual arousal and sexual responding. Yet, the women in this study *reported* a heightened sense of sexual arousal as they consumed more and more alcohol! Men are notorious for their sexual advances and heightened sexual interests after drinking. Indeed, a significant percentage of males are convinced that they are better lovers and much more amorous when they imbibe. Yet, their wives and lovers are often quick to point out the truth of this matter! Lost erections, delayed ejaculation or the inability to ejaculate, premature ejaculation, impotence, or complete amensia (blackout) for a sexual encounter can be the direct result of episodic or chronic alcohol abuse by men. Male alcoholics consistently report that they have spent many evenings "romancing" or attempting to seduce a willing partner, only to wake up the next morning and not know if they were "successful" or not. No doubt, many women have had similar experiences.

It is also important to point out that alcohol use may in fact enhance the sexual responding of some individuals and/or couples. This is a very sensitive issue and a reality that has been overgeneralized and distorted for hundreds of years by people in virtually all societies. Small doses of ethanol can delay the ejaculatory response of some male premature ejaculators. Ethanol may also help some men and women overcome their sexual inhibitions and fears. Likewise, alcohol may partially block or extinguish the sexual performance anxiety of select women and men. I treated a woman several years ago who reported that intercourse was always painful unless she consumed "two or three *stiff ones*" before initiating sexual activity. Thus, in some cases a small or moderate amount of alcohol may actually enhance sexual responding.

The faux pas in these situations where alcohol use does positively facilitate sexual responding rests with the process of relying upon a chemical solution to relationship and communication problems. The vast majority of sexual problems are in reality basic communication and relationship disturbances. Sexually inhibited individuals or premature ejaculators need to develop relationship, communication, and sexual behavioral skills that help them overcome or modify their maladaptive patterns of sexual responding. They don't need whiskey or beer to help them change their patterns of sexual responding! Furthermore, ethanol-induced solutions to sexual problems do not work in the long run. Drinking to cope with human sexual problems eventually results in more problems—problems in all areas of human functioning!

Thus, the realities of alcohol use and sexual responding are many and complex. Alcohol can inhibit sexual responding and contribute to various sexual disorders and problems. However, in a minority of situations limited alcohol use may temporarily enhance sexual responding.

WHAT ABOUT ALCOHOL, INTIMACY, AND ROMANCE?

What about booze and romance or booze and intimate human encounters? Most people somehow associate drinking and romance. Think about the following associations for a few seconds: a romantic meal with wine, cocktails for two, toast the bride, bread, good wine and a lover, and drinks with a special person after the game. The fact is that Americans associate drinking with courtship, dating, marriage, and even extramarital affairs. In short, we believe that alcohol is a magical or integral component in all forms of intimate, romantic, sexual, and loving behavior!

The media reinforce and shape our beliefs and perceptions about drinking, romance, and intimacy. Television and movie characters often have a drink in their hands and they clearly and consistently "mix" alcohol with their love scenes, sexual encounters, and affairs. The daily "soaps" abound in behaviors, themes, and passions that are soaked in ethanol. Our national football, baseball, boxing, basketball, and tennis heroes share with us the many and diversified benefits of drinking certain brands of beer every fifteen or twenty minutes, every hour of the day, on every TV channel available to the viewer! Furthermore, these internationally famous athletic stars overtly and covertly tell the viewing audience that alcohol enhances their sexuality, romantic inclinations, and seductive abilities!

In short, the "romantic American" is usually a drinker or perceived to be a drinker. When it comes to matters of sex, romance, and alcohol we know that "candy is dandy, but liquor is quicker." Alcohol does enable people to overcome some of their sexual inhibitions and thus sometimes acts to foster sexual relations. The fact is that alcohol is generally a disinhibitor. After a few drinks virtually all people behave in a generally less-inhibited fashion. Certainly, college-age males have been aware of these realities for decades, if not centuries, and based upon this awareness they have been quick to provide their dates with "a few" drinks.

It was pointed out earlier in this chapter that heavy drinking and alcohol abuse cause sexual responding problems. Likewise, alcohol abuse is a deterrent to intimate and romantic human relating. Alcoholism is a disorder of intimacy. The simple fact is that alcohol misuse causes major intimacy problems for thousands of couples. Intoxicated individuals are unable to be intimate, loving, and romantic in a healthy fashion. The authentic, genuine, and sharing dimensions of truly intimate and loving human encounters are distorted and "blocked" by alcohol misuse. An intoxicated person is unable to experience, share, and express authentic feelings of intimacy and romance. Heavy drinkers are unable to be intimate with self or others. It is virtually impossible to be intimate, loving, and romantic with another human being in the absence of an integrated, intimate, and sober relationship with self.

Alcoholics and alcohol abusers are people who are out of touch with their innermost feelings. They are afraid of intimacy and they tend to deny and repress feelings that are associated with intimacy. Paradoxically, these individuals use ethanol in order to *appear* to be intimate, romantic, and loving. Drinking enables them to overcome their fears of intimacy. Through the medium of intoxication these people create a false self that appears to be loving and feeling oriented. Yet, the addict is always out of touch with his or her real needs for intimate relating. In the absence of drinking, the addict is frightened or even terrified by feelings, self-awareness, and intimate relationships. Tragically, such individuals are literally "starved" for love, intimacy, and romance; yet, they are unable to express, share, and meet these basic needs within the context of their relationships with self and significant others. It is not surprising that they eventually turn to alcohol and other mood-altering chemicals in order to somehow meet their powerful needs for intimacy and relatedness.

In spite of the many conflictual aspects of alcohol misuse and our basic human needs for intimacy, love and romance, the fact remains that most people somehow associate alcohol use with sex and intimate human relations. In fact, most of these people also are not alcoholics and they do not misuse alcohol within the contexts of their sexual or intimate and romantic encounters. Unlike alcoholics and addicts, they do not *need* to ingest mood-altering chemicals in order to be feeling, loving, romantic, and intimate human beings. They do not feel "driven" or compelled to use drugs or alcohol for sexual or relationship purposes.

For many people a glass of wine within the context of a special relationship or romantic occasion is not problematic. Indeed, a drink or two may seem to enhance the romantic atmosphere. One or two drinks do not actually *make* people more romantic, intimate, or loving, but a small amount of alcohol may contribute to the development of an atmosphere in which feelings of warmth, relaxation, and closeness can be experienced and openly shared. In sum, limited alcohol use upon the part of healthy individuals who are involved in healthy and loving relationships may result in enhanced feelings of romance, sexuality, and intimacy. Psychologically, these individuals and couples are able to maintain a responsible and healthy *alcohol-relationship mix* rather than merely an *alcohol-sex* mix! Alcohol is not an essential or even important aspect of their relationships. They may periodically ingest alcoholic beverages within the context of their relationship, but they do not need to drink in order to have intimate, loving, healthy, and romantic involvements.

GUIDELINES FOR RESPONSIBLE ALCOHOL USE WITHIN THE CONTEXTS OF INTIMATE, SEXUAL, AND ROMANTIC RELATIONSHIPS

Alcohol use can be a relatively unimportant and also non-pathological component of many loving, romantic, intimate human relationships. These loving and in-depth human relationships may involve husbands and wives, lovers, parents, adult children, or close friends. However, there are guidelines which determine the parameters of responsible and healthy alcohol use within the framework of in-depth relationships. These guidelines include:

(1) The drinking behaviors of each person involved in such a relationship are clearly not abusive or pathological, and as such,
(2) Alcohol use is simply not important to the initiation and/or maintenance of the relationship,

(3) The relationship per se is healthy, in-depth, intimate, loving, romantic, and sexual or sensual,
(4) Alcohol is not used to facilitate the expression of sexual intimacy, nor is alcohol used as an agent to cope with sexual dysfunctions or sexually oriented relationship problems,
(5) Alcohol use is limited and infrequent within the contexts of intimate, romantic, sexual, and loving human interactions, and
(6) The individuals involved in such in-depth relationships consistently adhere to these guidelines and they also tend to simultaneously perceive the importance of maintaining the guidelines.

These basic guidelines are constructed around the belief that an in-depth and healthy relationship is the essential precursor to a healthy sexual relationship. Alcohol and sex per se is a highly combustible "mix" as well as a potentially dangerous or irresponsible mix. This is particularly true when alcohol and sex are "mixed" in the absence of a loving, romantic, and intimate relationship.

Sexual relationships that involve genuine intimacy, love, and romance between two essentially healthy human beings do not encompass heavy drinking or alcohol abuse upon the part of the persons involved in these relationships. Alcohol is not an important ingredient in these relationships, and the individuals in these relationships drink very little or choose not to imbibe. Such couples are essentially healthy and full-functioning, both as individuals and as couples.

People who drink responsibly within the context of a healthy and loving relationship do not need to drink in order to be intimate, sexual, or sensual. These individuals do not use ethanol to help them express their sexuality. In fact, many of these individuals consciously choose to keep alcohol out of the bedroom and out of their sexual relationships. They understand the "risks" of bringing whiskey or beer into their bedrooms! They are not desirous of entering a ménage à trois that involves ethanol as a third person.

Most people have experienced some degree or type of sexual dysfunction or sexual problem within the contexts of marriage and loving. However, it is important for people to realize that drinking is never a rational, healthy, or long-term solution for any sexual dysfunction or sexual problem. Alcohol use usually exacerbates sexual problems. Sometimes, drinking enables people to deny, distort, or rationalize a sexual problem, but the fact remains that drinking is not a *solution* for sexual difficulties.

With all of these caveats surrounding the alcohol and sex issue in mind, let me again point out that there is such a "thing" as responsible alcohol use within the contexts of intimate, romantic, and sexual relationships. The key to responsible drinking within the context of any human relationship and especially a sexual relationship is that the individuals in these relationships behave in accord with the six guidelines presented in this chapter. Alcohol is not an important ingredient in healthy human relationships, and human beings do not enhance their sexual responding via imbibing. Indeed, whenever an individual or couple must drink in order to attempt to be romantic, intimate, loving, or sexual, that person or couple is in trouble!

The fact is that thousands of couples experience a diversity of sexual problems and romantic disappointments as a result of alcohol abuse. Alcohol abuse causes intimacy problems as well as the fear of sexual intercourse. Drunks are usually lousy lovers! They sometimes stink, their actual foreplay and sexual techniques are often nonexistent, they have performance problems, and sometimes they can't even remember what they did the next morning! Obviously, irresponsible drinking causes sexual problems.

A final guideline for women drinkers: *never* drink when pregnant. Even seemingly small amounts of alcohol consumed during pregnancy can cause fetal alcohol syndrome (FAS). Infants who are born with FAS manifest learning difficulties, physical abnormalities, lower birthweight, and other health complications. Women also need to be aware of the effects and relationships between alcohol use and their menstrual cycles. Some women report that they actually drink more and/or crave alcohol some three to seven days prior to their period.

SUMMARY

Human beings have a long history of using ethanol for a diversity of sexually oriented purposes. Throughout time and in nearly every culture, people have experimented with every possible "mix" of alcohol and sex. Many people drink in order to express their sexual feelings, impulses, and desires.

Some people believe that alcohol is a magical sexual elixir or love potion. Many people do learn to utilize ethanol as a sexual disinhibitor. In part, these individuals become pathologically dependent upon the disinhibiting effects of drinking on sexual behavior. These individuals do perceive alcohol and/or other drugs as love potions or elixirs when their sexual responding seems to be chemically enhanced. The simple truth of this matter is that alcohol and/or other drugs are not love potions!

It was emphasized in this chapter that alcohol use does not generally enhance sexual functioning and sexual responding. To the contrary, alcohol abuse and even small amounts of ethanol use can cause or contribute to the development of a diversity of sexual dysfunction problems. Alcohol abuse and alcohol dependence are also associated with deviant sexual acting-out. While many men and women believe that their sexual responding is enhanced by alcohol use, the research evidence clearly suggests that male and female sexual responding is generally impaired or diminished by drinking. Thus, drinking can contribute to the development of such sexual problems as impotence, painful coitus, premature ejaculation, retarded ejaculation, and anorgasmia.

Booze can also become a deterrent to genuine human intimacy and relating. It was noted in this chapter that romance, intimacy, and in-depth relationships and love are the essential precursors to exciting and healthy sex. While limited and infrequent alcohol use may psychologically make some individuals or couples feel more romantic, loving, or sexual, the fact remains: alcohol and drinking do not *make* people more loving, sensuous, or romantic. Happy and healthy couples may drink for seemingly romantic reasons, but they do not *need* alcohol in order to be intimate or romantic, show feelings, or express their sexuality. Healthy and loving relationships involve individuals who are not dependent upon ethanol as an agent of relationship enhancement.

Several guidelines were presented in this chapter for responsible drinking within the contexts of intimate, loving, sexual relationships. These guidelines also encompass the various parameters of responsible alcohol use that were discussed in earlier chapters. Guideline number four is of particular importance and relevance to the content of the present chapter: alcohol is not used to facilitate the expression of sexual intimacy, nor is alcohol used as an agent to cope with sexual dysfunctions or sexually oriented relationship problems. Loving and healthy individuals may choose to periodically share a drink or two as a part of their romantic or sensual experiences. Such individuals do not drink heavily or attempt to get their loved one drunk in order to be loving or have sex.

In addition to the guidelines presented in this chapter, it is important for the reader to bear in mind that it is generally wise to keep alcohol out of the bedroom. Alcohol and sex do not mix! In reality, the alcohol-sex mix is a destructive and highly combustible mix for hundreds of thousands of Americans on an annual if not daily basis.

The destructive and irresponsible effects of mixing alcohol and sex are well known but generally not discussed. Marital infidelity and sexual acting-out are frequently alcohol-facilitated. The initial sexual experiences of over 70 percent of teenagers are alcohol-facilitated. No doubt, hundreds of thousands of unwanted pregnancies occur each year as a result of the alcohol-sex mix. Thousands of abortions are performed in this country each year as a result of unwanted pregnancies that are alcohol-related. There is no way to accurately learn how many thousands of spontaneous miscarriages take place as a result of alcohol misuse. Birth defects and fetal alcohol syndrome are caused by drinking. Finally, a diversity of sexually transmitted diseases are associated with alcohol misuse. How many men and women contract genital lice, genital herpes, gonorreah, AIDS or other sexually transmitted diseases each year as a result of alcohol-facilitated sexual relations?

The facts are very clear and simple: alcohol and sex do not mix. Responsible alcohol use can be one unimportant aspect of dating, romance, and courtship between two healthy individuals involved in a healthy relationship. Healthy couples do not need or want alcohol involved in their intimate, sensual, sexual encounters. These couples realize the risks of involving ethanol in their relationships. They simply value each other and their relationships to the extent that they are unwilling to risk the negative consequences of mixing alcohol with their sexuality.

Chapter 12

WHAT ABOUT ALCOHOL AND OTHER DRUGS?

CHEMICAL SOLUTIONS: LIVING BETTER THROUGH MODERN CHEMISTRY?

We live in a world that revolves around the uses and abuses of thousands of mood-altering chemicals. Think about the myriad chemical solutions modern science has developed for the simple aches and pains of life! There are literally dozens of chemical remedies or solutions for the everyday headache. Indeed, we are confronted with the task of choosing between such chemical remedies as aspirin, Bufferin, Nuprin, Tylenol, Anacin, and probably ten or fifteen other over-the-counter medications for a simple headache. If these "drugs" do not sufficiently relieve our headache or pain, we can obtain a prescription for any one of several stronger and more potent medications from our family physician.

Through modern chemistry and pharmacology we have developed chemical solutions for virtually all of life's problems, aches and pains, and discomforts. In truth, many of these derived solutions for living problems work and many do not work or at best cause some degree of positive placebo effect. Unfortunately, there are also adverse side effects or negative consequences associated with taking many seemingly harmless drugs.

The most widely used and abused chemical solution for all of mankind's living problems has always been and probably always will be alcohol. Like many of the modern chemical solutions for living problems, alcohol also "works." The basic fact is that alcohol "works" or seems to alleviate and somehow alter many of the aches and pains of daily living, both physical and psychological! Ethanol is a cheap, easy, readily accessible, fast-acting, legal, and socially acceptable chemical solution to many of our daily living problems. Furthermore, the recent technologies of the brewing and liquor industries have created a diversity of new, sweeter, different, better, and more exciting alcoholic beverages. Alcohol is believed to be such an effective chemical solution for depression, stress, financial problems, work difficulties, marital conflicts, health problems, and death or simply living, that we are willing to spend millions and millions of our hard-earned dollars for this substance. Thus, it is certainly not surprising that the manufacturers of alcoholic beverages can earn billions of dollars every year selling, developing, and marketing these "chemical solutions" to you and I.

During the past four decades we have greatly expanded our repertoire of chemical solutions for psychologically oriented problems. Indeed, modern chemistry and psychopharmacology have contributed to the development of hundreds of new chemical remedies for anxiety and stress, depression, confused thinking, and virtually every variety of human emotional discomfort and suffering. Modern chemistry enables us to speed up, slow down, sleep, remain awake, feel no pain, think clearer, and so forth.

People do not like to feel or experience any form of emotional discomfort. We want to be at our emotional best all of the time, and most of us do not have the time or the patience to be anxious or even situationally upset. Just as we want to be young, attractive, strong, and physically healthy, we also want to feel psychologically strong, alert, and exuberant all of the time. Many people feel deeply frustrated when they experience any conscious form of emotional discomfort.

In addition to these realities, hundreds of thousands of people do experience significant clinical depressions, anxiety and panic attacks of various types, impulse control problems, schizophrenia, brain disorders, and a diversity of neurotic problems. Millions of people do in fact suffer with various types and degrees of psychiatric/psychological problems. Thus, it should not be surprising that the wonders of modern pharmacology include "psychotropic" drugs that attempt to provide chemical solutions for these various psychiatric and psychological problems. Like ethanol, many of these psychotropic drugs do "work," while others may not work or have questionable therapeutic efficacy. These drugs also tend to be relatively fast-acting, inexpensive, socially acceptable, legal, and prescribed by physicians. Some of these medications are highly addictive as well as potentially toxic or life-threatening when taken in high doses or over a period of extended usage. The various tranquilizers and painkillers are particularly addictive and subject to abuse and addiction.

Modern chemistry has also contributed to the development of a diversity of illicit or illegal drugs that are taken by millions of people. These illicit drugs are used to change feelings, perceptions, relax, speed up, and for the other reasons that were discussed earlier in the contexts of alcohol use and prescription drug use. The late 1960s marked the beginning of the legal as well as illicit "drug revolution." The widespread use of marijuana, psychedelic drugs, "uppers and downers," cocaine, and even the so-called "designer drugs" actually began during the late 1960s and early 1970s. In recent years, "street pharmacists" or "street chemists" as well as bona fide laboratory scientists have developed new mood-altering drugs and even new methods of ingesting these chemicals. For example, a few years ago a hallucinogenic drug called "blotter acid" became available to teenagers on the streets, and this chemical could be taken by eating small pieces of paper that were drug-soaked or by simply placing these pieces of paper against the skin.

Each year brings about the development and availability of new and usually very addictive, dangerous illicit drugs. The "new" heroin or "black tar" from Mexico is said to be over 40 times more potent than the heroin that is usually available on the streets of all metropolitan areas. "Ecstasy" replaces "angel dust" or "STP" and so it goes—one drug perpetually replaces another on the evolving current list of "favorite" or most widely abused illicit drugs. Certainly cocaine and cocaine derivatives such as "crack" are the most popular and "trendy" illicit drugs of choice today. Thousands of Americans use and become abusers of cocaine daily. However, cocaine is only the "in" drug of today. Within several months or a few years there will be many other addictive drugs that will be popular and abused by many. The deaths and myriad problems that are created through the uses of these chemicals seem to be somehow unimportant or overlooked. We are a chemical society that demands chemical solutions to all living problems—at any price!

IF ONE IS GOOD, THEN TWO MUST BE BETTER: THE ALCOHOL-DRUG MIX MENTALITY

The mentality or belief system that reinforces alcohol abuse and alcohol dependence is simply "more than one is better, if not absolutely necessary." This same general style of thinking permeates our collective American pattern of using or abusing all varieties of medications and chemicals. We seem to behave and believe in excess! One or two of anything is frequently not enough.

Thus, an emergent characteristic of American drug-taking behavior is simply that of combining alcohol with various other mood-altering drugs. We tend to smoke "pot" while drinking wine or other alcoholic beverages. Some people ingest amphetamines in the morning in order to "get going" and then take barbiturates, drink, or narcotics in the evening to "come down." Thousands of people rely upon medications each night for inducing sleep and then consume cup after cup of coffee during the day in order to remain aware and alert. Millions of drug abusers ingest "coke," "speed," alcohol, and smoke marijuana *together* and on a regular basis! Indeed, chemical-dependency treatment programs are filled with people who are *polydrug* dependent or polydrug abusers. These individuals will literally ingest any and/or all drugs that somehow change their mood, emotions, perceptions, and being.

The emergent pattern of mixing alcohol with various other mood-altering chemicals is really quite apparent in the United States. Furthermore, this general pattern encompasses the use and abuse of all varieties of drugs—legal or illicit drugs, over-the-counter medications, and prescription drugs. Many individuals think nothing of having "a couple of drinks" in combination with an antibiotic medication or perhaps even with a steroid or blood pressure medication. In fact, I have treated hundreds of patients who have been taking physician-prescribed hypertensive medications and drinking a fifth of vodka or whiskey each day, every day, for several years! Needless to say, over half of these patients no longer required hypertensive medication shortly after they stopped drinking and were in therapy and involved in a program of recovery.

Some individuals go from doctor to doctor to get pills and medications for "stress," headaches or backaches, depression, and every imaginable malaise. Unfortunately, a few doctors are all too ready to supply these people with their magical chemical solutions. Economic realities shape and influence all of these processes. Alcohol and other drugs can be a cheap (or relatively inexpensively *perceived*) solution for any living problem. Doctors know or believe that many drugs are quick, easy, and inexpensive solutions to pain and human suffering. None of us like or enjoy pain and apparent suffering. Pharmaceutical companies want to help sick people, doctors want to help sick people, bartenders and drug dealers usually want to help their "clients," people in general want to help themselves feel less anxious and "better," and above all, the dollar and cents rewards for this game are tremendous for nearly all of the participants! The pharmaceutical companies are paid billions of dollars each year for developing, manufacturing, and selling drugs to combat every form of human suffering. Physicians are paid billions of dollars each year for writing prescriptions for the chemicals and drugs that the pharmaceutical companies manufacture and sell. Finally, the illicit drug industry is the largest and most profitable business in the world! The number-one cash crop in the United States is marijuana, not corn, wheat, or potatoes. State and local police as well as federal drug administration agents confiscate millions of dollars' worth of cocaine, "pot," and other illicit drugs each day in this country. Liquor stores, bars, and the liquor industry legally sell and distribute millions of dollars worth of the most widely used and abused drug in the world on a daily basis!

In short, we ingest over-the-counter drugs with alcohol, mix ethanol with illicit drugs, drink in combination with prescription medications, and literally consume and develop more and more mood-altering chemicals each day. Most people seem to be oblivious to the risks associated with "mixing" and the "more is better" mentality and life-style.

RISK FACTORS ASSOCIATED WITH MIXING ALCOHOL AND OTHER DRUGS

The National Safety Council reports (1986) that the misuse of medicines and over-the-counter medications such as aspirin accounts for 40 percent of the some two million accidental poisonings that take place each year in this country! Furthermore, the victims of such accidental poisonings usually mix a drug or several drugs with alcohol. They mix drugs that have a depressant effect on the central nervous system with ethanol which is also a central nervous system depressant.

Perhaps most people do not realize that mixing even commonly prescribed medications or over-the-counter drugs with fruit or vegetable juice can be extremely hazardous to the health of some people! The medicine or drug-alcohol mix can be and all too frequently is deadly. Consider the following consequences of mixing alcohol with several commonly used medicines: alcohol can dissolve the outer coating of timed-release pills (cold medications, diet pills) and potentially result in a large, single, toxic overdose; alcohol in combination with blood pressure medication can cause low as well as fluxuating blood pressure; alcohol reduces or eliminates the effect of antibiotic medications; alcohol in combination with aspirin can irritate the stomach and cause internal hemorrhaging; alcohol in combination with psychotropic medication (tranquilizers, antidepressants, and antipsychotics) can facilitate agitation, lethargy, mental confusion, or stupor; and alcohol and certain cough medicines can severely depress the central nervous system and result in stupor or even death. These are but a few of the hazards of mixing alcohol and commonly used medicines.

Whenever alcohol is combined with any drug or psychoactive chemical it is possible that these substances will potentiate each other. Thus, alcohol may significantly affect the manner in which any given drug acts in your body. This process has been referred to as "drug interaction effect." Moreover, whenever two or more drugs are taken simultaneously one can synergistically compound the effects of the other so that the overall drug-induced outcome is far more acute or radical than if the two drugs were taken separately. The simple equation in terms of physical and/or psychological outcome of mixing drugs is not $1 + 1 = 2$, but rather $1 + 1 = 3, 5, 10$ or some other synergized outcome effect. It can be difficult, if not impossible, to consistently predict the effect of mixing alcohol with various other drugs. However, the more drugs or medications that a person combines, the greater the chances of experiencing a drug interaction effect.

There are many risks associated with mixing alcohol and "pot," cocaine, "speed," "downers," narcotics, and other illicit drugs as well as physician-prescribed mood-altering chemicals. Cocaine use alone can result in cardiac arrest, irregular heartbeat, and other medical problems. Many "coke" addicts use alcohol as a depressant to "come down" after a "coke run." Amphetamine abusers use alcohol for the same purpose. The synergistic effects of mixing ethanol with any of these substances can be devastating and life-threatening. The combination of any two or more of these drugs significantly and negatively affects judgment, reasoning, motor skills, perception, and basic bodily functioning. Mixing ethanol with barbiturates ("downers"), narcotics, or tranquilizers can literally slow the human heart and respiratory system down to the point of inducing death! Smoking "pot" and drinking while driving is often a fatal and always doubly dangerous mix.

Alcohol and drug treatment centers are filled with people who are "dual-addicted," or polydrug abusers and addicts. These individuals are addicted to more than one mood-altering drug. Many patients in chemical dependency treatment centers are addicted to alcohol and marijuana, alcohol and cocaine, or alcohol, painkillers, tranquilizers, and virtually any other addictive substance. These people "mix" alcohol and drugs to the extent of developing multiple drug addictions. Many recovering addicts have a history of "switching" addictions. For example, such a person might enter a treatment program for alcoholism, attend AA, and remain totally abstinent from ethanol but initiate a pattern of daily marijuana or other drug dependence shortly after sobering up. Eventually, these persons discover that mixing or switching addictive drugs does not work. Recovery from polydrug addiction begins when the addict is able to make and keep a commitment to a *totally* drug-free life-style.

GUIDELINES FOR RESPONSIBLE ALCOHOL-DRUG MIXING

It should be apparent to the reader that any alcohol-other drug mix is risky or potentially dangerous. Thus, the most prudent guideline for responsible alcohol-drug mixing is simply "don't." Alcohol should not be combined with other medicines, illicit drugs, or even prescribed drugs. It is simply risky and therefore potentially irresponsible to mix alcohol with aspirin, blood pressure medication, marijuana or cocaine, tranquilizers, "sleeping pills," narcotics, or any other substance that affects the structure and/or functioning of the human body. Alcohol does not mix well with a diversity of medicines. The safest and most responsible rule is to avoid drinking whenever taking *any kind* of over-the-counter medication or prescription drug.

The risks associated with mixing alcohol and illicit drugs are generally greater than those associated with mixing alcohol with over-the-counter medicines and prescription drugs. There is no way to know the precise ingredients in any "street" drug. Whenever a person buys marijuana, cocaine, or some other illicit drug from a "friend" or street dealer he or she never really knows what substances are actually in the drug. Furthermore, the psychoactive drugs are more likely than over-the-counter drugs to synergize and potentiate each other when mixed. Thus, mixing alcohol with illicit and/or psychoactive drugs can be double-trouble.

More and more physicians are advising their patients to avoid mixing alcohol with any and all other medications or drugs. Indeed, most people are beginning to realize and accept that it is both risky and irresponsible to mix alcohol with other drugs. Drug-alcohol mixes can jeopardize the health and well-being of the user as well as significant others and society.

The following guidelines may help minimize some of the risks that are associated with mixing prescribed medications and/or over-the-counter drugs. Again, these *drugs* should *not* be mixed with ethanol.

(1) Whenever your family physician prescribes a medication or over-the-counter drug, be sure to let him or her know if you are taking other medications or drugs.
(2) Ask your doctor what the precautions are, side effects, or drug interaction effects of the medications that he or she prescribes for you; in other words, don't be afraid to ask questions and make every effort to communicate about these issues with your doctor.
(3) *Read the labels* and precautions on all over-the-counter drugs and prescribed medications that you take.
(4) Follow the instructions on the label. In other words, take the prescribed dosage, when and how it is prescribed on the label.
(5) Follow all warnings on the label. Remember, warnings are based upon research evidence and they are included on the label to protect the consumer—you!
(6) Follow your doctor's advice when it comes to the prescription drugs—take medications according to your doctor's guidelines.

Finally, it is important to realize that the effectiveness of any drug or over-the-counter medication is largely determined by you. Think about this. How you take a drug determines how it works. For example, if your physician prescribes an antibiotic medication three times a day for a period of seven days and you only take the medication once a day for three days, it is reasonable to expect that the medication will not "work." You are ultimately responsible for the decision to mix or not mix alcohol and other drugs, and you are also largely responsible for the consequences or outcome of taking a drug.

A final word of caution. If you aren't a physician, don't give your prescription drugs to another person! Not only is this risky business, it is irresponsible and even illegal. If you are giving your child or loved one an over-the-counter medication or a physician-prescribed medication, follow the guidelines that were just delineated. It is important for all of us to realize that we teach and model responsible or irresponsible alcohol-drug taking behaviors in all of our alcohol-other drug related interactions with children and significant others.

SUMMARY

We live in an alcohol and other drug oriented society and world. Modern pharmacology has developed chemical solutions for every ailment known to mankind. There are drugs and chemical solutions for pain, headaches, backaches, depression, stress and anxiety, confused thinking, sleep disorders, and even flatulence. The most widely used and abused chemical solution for all of these human ailments has historically been ethanol. Hundreds of "new" over-the-counter drugs, prescription medications, and illicit drugs are developed each year for any and all possible types of human living problems.

As we continue to develop new and often more potent drugs to remedy these different human maladies, we have also initiated a cultural pattern of polydrug consumption. Americans tend to be multiple drug consumers. We take antibiotics for a sinus infection, antihistamines to help us breathe, vitamin C to fight the cold, and aspirin for the pain—all at once! The basic logic or mentality that supports this pattern of behavior is "if one is good, two are better." This mentality applies to all types of drug-taking behavior. Thus, illicit drug abusers and addicts frequently "do" cocaine, drink alcohol, and smoke "pot" at the same time! More and more people who enter chemical dependency treatment programs are polydrug-dependent. Counselors and therapists in these treatment centers wonder whatever happened to the "pure alcoholics"? Smoking cigarettes, drinking coffee, and ingesting any other or several other mood-altering chemicals with ethanol has become another American "way of life."

Several risk factors associated with mixing alcohol and other drugs were discussed in this chapter. Drug mixing can be hazardous to your health! Taking more than one drug at a time can result in a "drug interaction effect." Quite simply, this means that drugs can interact with each other and the human body in an unpredictable manner. Many drugs interactively synergize or potentiate each other. It is always risky to drink alcohol when taking time-released pills, blood pressure medications, antibiotics, aspirin, barbiturates, narcotics, or any psychotropic medication. Mixing such illicit drugs as "coke" or "crack," "pot," "speed," "psychedelics," or "downers" together or with ethanol is extremely dangerous and irrational.

It was stressed in this chapter that *any* alcohol-other drug mix is risky or potentially dangerous. Therefore, the most important guideline for mixing alcohol and other drugs is "don't"! The most responsible solution to the issue of combining alcohol with other drugs is simply not to engage in this practice. More and more physicians are telling their patients not to mix alcohol with prescribed medications and other drugs. In fact, the reader should consult his or her family physician about the potentiating or synergistic effects of mixing a prescribed medication or medications with any over-the-counter drugs that he or she might be taking.

Six guidelines were presented in this chapter to help the reader reduce the risks that are associated with mixing prescribed medications and/or over-the-counter drugs. It is important to communicate openly and honestly with your physician about all kinds of drugs and their effects. It is also very important to read the labels and follow the instructions that are on the labels of all over-the-counter drugs. Likewise, follow your doctor's advice and guidelines when it comes to taking any prescription drug.

Finally, it is important to realize that you are basically responsible for the effects and effectiveness of any drug. How the drug is taken, in what amount, when, and so forth are ultimately the responsibilities of the person taking any drug or drugs. Never mix ethanol with other drugs, and only take these drugs when it is absolutely necessary. Chemical solutions for living problems always involve some degree of risk, and the "more's better" mentality is even more risky!

Chapter 13

TEACHING RESPONSIBLE ALCOHOL USE BEHAVIORS AND HELPING IRRESPONSIBLE DRINKERS

SUGGESTIONS FOR TEACHING RESPONSIBLE ALCOHOL USE BEHAVIORS

The belief that people can be taught to drink responsibly is based upon the premise that it is possible to consume ethanol in a responsible manner. The various parameters of responsible drinking were delineated in Chapters 2 and 4 of this book. It may be helpful for the reader to reread these particular chapters as he or she considers the content and concepts included in the present chapter.

It has been my practical as well as clinical observation over the past thirty years that most drinkers do not become alcoholics or severe alcohol abusers. These individuals are responsible drinkers as defined in Chapter 4 and they have obviously somehow learned to drink responsibly. How do they differ from alcoholics and problem drinkers, and how do these people learn to be responsible drinkers? Why can't alcoholic persons learn to consume alcohol responsibly? While the answers to these questions are complex, multifaceted, and unclear, it is apparent that learning is one important variable that affects the manner in which any person uses alcohol. Alcoholics may be unable to drink responsibly because they have an uncurable disease or because their brain chemistries differ significantly from so-called "normal" drinkers. Nonetheless, addicts also learn and teach themselves to be alcohol or other drug dependent. Learning, conditioning, and reinforcement are factors that affect or shape all forms of behavior, including alcoholism and alcoholic patterns of behavior! Likewise, learning factors also play important roles in the development of social drinking or various patterns of non-problematic alcohol consumption.

Think about the myriad ways in which *learning* influences and shapes all of our lives. Indeed, human beings learn to drive automobiles and airplanes, eat select foods at certain times of the day, brush their teeth or use a particular brand of toothpaste, go to select stores in order to buy groceries or clothes, add and subtract, and so forth. We literally must learn every thought, behavior, act, or skill that becomes a part of our self-experience repertoire. As surely as each of us must learn to walk and talk, we also learn to drink milk, tea, or a particular alcoholic beverage.

An incredible amount of learning is involved in the simple process of imbibing. Adolescents tell each other that they must "acquire a taste" for a certain alcoholic beverage or "learn to like" the taste of beer. The connoisseur of fine wines spends many years learning to identify the different tastes and even smells of different wines. Drinkers learn to "mix" different kinds of alcoholic drinks, and it is essential to even learn where to go in order to purchase alcoholic beverages. It is important to learn how to open a beer can or how much it costs to purchase different alcoholic beverages. In sum, a diversity of learning factors interactively determine and shape the alcohol use or non-use behaviors of each individual.

Learning can occur in several different ways. For example, human beings learn from direct experience, practice, observation, accident, trial and error, and reading. However, a great deal of learning takes place as a result of teaching. Human beings spend a great deal of time and effort teaching each other how to live more efficiently. Teaching and learning are generally goal-directed or purposive activities. Thus, teachers tell and show their students how to solve math problems. Parents attempt to verbally teach their children how to behave in accord with culturally and socially defined norms. Parents also attempt to "set the example" for their children. Parental behaviors demonstrate and show children how to behave. This form of teaching involves imitative learning and modeling.

Teaching and learning are also very complex processes. Students and children don't always learn what their teachers and parents attempt to teach them, and everyone differs in learning and teaching skills as well as style. Educators and academicians have argued and debated for centuries about the most efficacious techniques or methods of instruction. Parents are notorious for their disagreements about how to teach or discipline sons and daughters. There are obviously many different ideas or viewpoints about how to teach young people or adults responsible alcohol use behaviors. Some might argue that all alcohol use is categorically irresponsible, and thus any technique or approach to teaching these behaviors would also be viewed as irresponsible. There are also people who believe that any use of ethanol by anyone will eventually lead to alcoholism or problematic drinking. These individuals no doubt attempt to teach others to abstain from all alcohol use. They also utilize various self-instruction and self-teaching techniques that are aimed at maintaining personal abstinence.

The general truth of this matter is that most parents utilize and attempt to employ a diversity of teaching techniques in their efforts to help children, significant others, and themselves drink responsibly. These teaching and educational techniques may be consciously thought out and planned or they may be unconsciously carried out. In reality, there is no single method for teaching people how to imbibe responsibly. Since any alcohol use can be risky, there are also no guarantees that an individual who has learned to drink responsibly at age thirty will not lose this ability by the age of forty or sixty-five. In spite of the many caveats surrounding the matter of teaching responsible alcohol use behaviors, there are a number of suggestions and guidelines that can be applied to this task. These suggestions and guidelines include:

(1) *Begin at home.* Attitudes, beliefs, feelings, and behaviors that involve alcohol use are shaped in the home environment. Parents need to begin teaching their children about alcohol use and other drugs when their children are only four or five years of age. Parents and significant others are the first and most important teachers and educators about alcohol use or other drugs. Alcohol education begins at home! Parents teach their children about alcohol and alcohol use vis-à-vis their personal alcohol use behaviors, patterns of consumption, as well as their attitudes, beliefs, feelings, values, and perceptions about ethanol. Parents and significant others are very powerful models. They are the child's first alcohol and drug educators! Indeed, the only form of alcohol use education that children receive before the age of five occurs at home. This education is provided by parents, family members, and significant others.

(2) *Begin early.* It was mentioned earlier that parental education and teaching methods shape and influence children's basic perceptions, attitudes, ideas, and beliefs about alcohol use and drinking. Parents need to begin educating their children about drinking and alcohol use when their children are three to five years of age. Parents need to maintain a consistent and open verbal dialogue with their children about drinking. This form of communicative interaction between parents and children should begin early in the parent-child relationship and encompasses the *duration* of the relationship.

School-based alcohol and drug education classes that are offered for junior high or senior high school students are literally "too little, too late." Furthermore, it is the *primary* responsibility of parents rather than schools to educate their children about alcohol use *within the home environment* and *early in life.*

(3) *Be consistent.* As touched upon earlier, it is not enough for parents to teach their children about alcohol and alcohol use during early childhood or some other relatively specific developmental era. Parents need to openly and consistently discuss alcohol use issues with their children throughout the course of their relationship. This dialogue is consistently maintained from the "cradle to the grave." Thus, parents need to consistently teach their children about alcohol and other drugs when their children are very young, when they are adolescents, and even when they are adults. Alcohol use education between parents and children does not end when children become adolescents or adults! It can be all too easy for us to forget that virtually anyone can develop a drinking problem at any age. There are no guarantees that young adults who do not abuse alcohol will not become alcohol abusers later in life. A consistent and lifelong focus upon the various aspects of drinking and alcohol use may help to minimize the risks of developing a drinking problem during any or all of the developmental life stages.

(4) *Focus on all issues associated with drinking and alcohol use.* It is not enough to simply tell and teach children to say no to alcohol and other drugs. Parents need to be knowledgeable about all aspects of ethanol use and drinking, and they need to teach their children about all of these issues at the age-appropriate time. While it is important for everyone to be able to assertively say no to alcohol and other drugs, it is eventually more important to fully understand why we choose to drink or not. It is important for children and adolescents to be familiar with the legal ramifications that are associated with drinking and other forms of chemical use. Parents need to help their children learn about the basics of alcohol use, abuse, addiction, peer pressure, and legal and social responsibility. Parents and teens need to be able to openly and consistently discuss the facts about drinking and driving, alcohol and other drugs, alcohol and sex or dating, possibly alcoholism or alcohol abuse in the family, depression and suicide, career development and work—in short, any and/or all issues that might be associated with drinking and alcohol use.

(5) *Encourage schools and educators to include didactic and experiential alcohol and drug education classes at every level of the educational curriculum.*

First and second grade students should be involved in alcohol/drug education classes as should junior high and senior high students. Every high school guidance counselor and school nurse or social worker should be able to provide didactic alcohol-drug education classes as well as conduct experiential groups to help students explore their beliefs, feelings, and choices about substance abuse. College and university counseling centers should routinely provide alcohol-drug education classes and programs as well as direct clinical services for students manifesting substance abuse oriented problems. Alcohol and other drug abuse education efforts are sporadic, inadequate, and inconsistent throughout the vast majority of school systems throughout the United States. Unfortunately, this reality applies to every level of our educational system—K through graduate school and medical school. Health professionals need to understand the fundamentals of alcohol and drug abuse as well as the parameters of responsible alcohol use. Parents and educators also need to clearly understand these issues.

(6) *Media educational efforts need to be directed toward the goal of making the general public much more aware of the parameters of responsible alcohol* use. For several decades, the media have been simply utilized only to reinforce alcohol use. Radio, television, and newspaper ads have historically been used to sell, market, and glamorize the consumption of alcoholic beverages. The liquor and media industries have not historically been concerned about educating the public about responsible alcohol use. They have been concerned primarily about the dollars and cents of selling and marketing ethanol. The responsible advertising, marketing, selling, and manufacturing of alcoholic beverages must consistently involve educating the public about (1) alcohol use, (2) the risks associated with alcohol use, misuse, and addiction, and (3) responsible alcohol use. A few of the major breweries have recently developed beer commercials for television that advocate moderate drinking and responsible use, i.e. not driving after drinking, etc. Television, radio, magazines, and newspapers need to be actively and consistently utilized to raise the general public's awareness and understanding about *all* facetsof drinking and alcohol use. Perhaps these potent reinforcers of social and personal behavior should not be utilized to sell or reinforce alcohol consumption?

(7) *Industry and the work environment should also be primary settings for ongoing alcohol and other drug education.* The job satisfaction and productivity of every employee is intricately associated with his or her health. As noted in earlier chapters, alcoholism and alcohol abuse

are major contributors to work problems of every imaginable variety. Certainly, alcohol abuse causes many health and emotional problems which in turn negatively affect job performance and work productivity. Employers need to provide continuous alcohol-drug education classes for all employees at every level of the corporate ladder. Employee assistance programs and personnel can provide this educational training as well as treatment services for impaired or dysfunctional employees. EAP personnel also need to clearly delineate corporate alcohol use policy and help all employees understand the nature of responsible alcohol use.

(8) *Finally, every clergyman, church, and religious group needs to be an alcohol educator!* Priests, pastors, nuns, Sunday school teachers, and the governing representatives of all denominations should be actively involved in the process of alcohol-drug education. Alcohol abuse and addiction problems erode the basic foundation of every institution in this country—even the church! Millions of people attend churches or maintain some form of meaningful religious affiliation. Thus, it is important for all religions to be vested in the process of educating parishioners about alcohol use. Since different religious denominations manifest different ideologies about alcohol use, it is only reasonable to expect that select religious groups might advocate total abstinence while others advocate alcohol use in moderation. Nonetheless, the teachers and leaders of all denominations need to be well-versed in all aspects of alcohol use, and this information should be rationally shared and taught within the structure of all church and religious groups. Traditional theological ideologies that fervently teach that any use of alcohol is evil or will lead to personal ruination or result in "going to hell" need to be replaced by rational ideology and educational methods that elucidate every facet of alcohol use—biologic and physiologic effects on the human body, use, abuse, and addiction, psychological effects of use, possible effects on the family, legal issues, social realities, and so forth. Historic religious dogma has not significantly reduced Western civilization's twenty-year alcohol and drug crisis. Prohibition has never been an effective long-term solution for the alcohol use problems of any society or culture. Religious groups need to consider turning their alcohol and drug education efforts away from the "total abstinence, hell fire and brimstone" model to a more rational, choice-oriented, responsible use-non-abuse or non-use model.

State and federal government health agencies also need to be actively involved in the process of educating the general public about responsible alcohol use. In sum, effective alcohol and drug education must take place at every level of society. Such a collective effort needs to be aimed at making the general public very cognizant of the parameters of responsible alcohol use as well as more accepting of the non-use alternative. Parents and families, schools, health educators and health providers, churches, government agencies, the media, and the liquor industry are the major alcohol use educators in America.

A major problem that will continue to undermine the most comprehensive and effective of alcohol education programs is the alcohol abuser. This is a systemic reality that has existed for decades, if not centuries. Hundreds of thousands of alcoholic or substance-abusing parents teach and tell their children not to drink or "take" drugs. Addicted doctors recommend that their patients attend Alcoholics Anonymous or enter a treatment program. Teachers and educators as well as priests and pastors warn their students or parishioners about the dangers of alcohol abuse, and yet thousands of these people are alcohol abusers. Star athletes and other role models warn teenagers about the hazards of alcohol and drug abuse, and yet everyday it seems as though another "star" is arrested, killed, or jailed as a result of substance abuse.

Let's face it, our society is very ambivalent about the uses and abuses of ethanol and other addictive substances. Police officers sometimes arrest "drug dealers" and then use, sell, or distribute the drugs they have confiscated from the "dealers" they have arrested! Government employees resent being forced to take random urine tests to detect drug use, and yet some of these people take drugs that do affect their job performance or even affect national security.

All of these inconsistencies and sources of ambivalence plus many more contribute to our difficulties in the realm of teaching responsible alcohol use behaviors. A major common denominator that actively contributes to all of the different problems that are associated with teaching responsible alcohol use behaviors is our collective struggle to deal with all aspects of responsible living. Americans are becoming progressively less willing to assume personal responsibility for their choices and actions in life. We are confused about behaving responsibly. We are also very ambivalent about responsible living. As we become a more compulsive, self-centered, action-oriented, "do-it-now" type of culture, we tend to shirk responsibility for our personal actions and expect others to somehow assume our responsibilities or we blame them for our mistakes and irresponsible acts. It seems to become easier to expect the boss, mayor, police—*others*—to be responsible for us.

Teaching responsible alcohol use behaviors needs to be an educational process that attempts to change attitudes, beliefs, perceptions, and emotions. The realities and facts of alcohol use and misuse are only one component of this educational model. Until alcohol and drug educators can impact their children's or students' basic values, attitudes, beliefs, perceptions, and feelings about alcohol or other drug use, they will only be minimally effective in their educational efforts. Long-term patterns of alcohol use—the drinking behaviors and pattern of consumption of individuals as well as groups or cultures—are the ultimate measures of the effectiveness of parents and programs that attempt to teach responsible alcohol use behaviors.

HELP FOR IRRESPONSIBLE DRINKERS

As noted throughout this book, hundreds of thousands of people in our country alone are unable to consistently drink ethanol in a responsible manner. There are a multiplicity of factors associated with this reality. Many people cannot drink responsibly simply because they have a disease called alcoholism which seems to preclude the possibility of social, controlled, or responsible drinking. There are people who behave irresponsibly in most or nearly all areas of their lives. It is not surprising that many of these people are not able to drink responsibly. Many people drink irresponsibly in order to cope with some major crisis in living, depression, a severe emotional or personality problem, or even brain damage. These people may eventually develop alcohol addiction. The causes of irresponsible drinking or even alcoholism are complex, individual in nature, and myriad.

There are several theories or ideas that attempt to explain why so many people do not drink responsibly. However, the fact is that these individuals do create tremendous problems for themselves, others, and society as a result of their abusive and destructive patterns of alcohol use. In the end, it makes very little difference why a given individual is unable to control his or her drinking. These people are in need of some form of help or intervention. The fact of the matter is that different types of irresponsible or abusive drinkers need different types of help. For example, alcoholics need to be involved in treatment and education programs that help them become and *remain* totally abstinent from alcohol. People who are arrested for drinking or using other drugs while driving need to be evaluated by an experienced health professional and placed in an appropriate education and/or treatment program. About one-third of these people are alcoholics and they should be referred to abstinence-oriented programs. The other two-thirds of this group need to be involved in counseling, prevention, and education programs. People who are periodically irresponsible drinkers also need to be involved in educational, rehabilitation, and counseling programs that are designed to meet their individual needs.

Perhaps the most important and yet often most difficult task facing the spouse, family, employer, or significant other of the irresponsible drinker is to get the drinker involved in some form of education or treatment program. Alcoholics and alcohol abusers are notorious for their inabilities to see and accept that they have drinking problems. They deny and distort the reality of their addictive illnesses. Indeed, it can be very difficult to get any irresponsible drinker to accept the reality that he or she is in fact not a responsible drinker.

The following guidelines are suggested as methods for initiating help for people who manifest *any* type of drinking problem. The reader might find it extremely helpful to read my earlier book, *How to Live with a Problem Drinker and Survive* (Forrest, 1986), if he or she needs to explore this issue in more depth:

(1) Make every effort to get the irresponsible drinker evaluated and into an appropriate treatment program or regimen.
(2) Don't neglect your own well-being. If you are living with a problem drinker, you also need to be involved in therapy, a self-help support group such as Al-Anon, and a program of recovery.
(3) Get help for yourself, even if the drinker denies that his or her drinking is problematic and therefore refuses to seek help or enter some form of treatment.
(4) Be consistent in your efforts to help yourself and the alcohol abuser in your life. Don't give up.
(5) Remember that serious alcohol-drug abuse problems usually do not magically go away without treatment. The incidence of "spontaneous remission" among alcohol-dependent persons is low.
(6) The "good news" is that at least 50–70 percent of even chronic alcoholics who receive any treatment evidence positive gains as a result of their treatment experiences, and

(7) Based upon this information, realistically expect the best. You can change and your drinker can recover!

As I have discussed in my earlier books, *How to Live with a Problem Drinker and Survive* and *How to Cope with a Teenage Drinker,* you will need to stop taking responsibility for the behaviors and actions of the irresponsible drinker in your life. You are not responsible for your drinker's alcoholism or problem drinking! Stop covering up, protecting, and alibiing for the drinker. Get out of the "protection racket." These are examples of enabling behavior on your part. These behaviors actually maintain and reinforce the drinker's pathologic style of consumption.

You will also find that the following suggestions can help you and the alcohol abuser in your life: Never allow yourself to be physically or verbally abused by the alcohol abuser in your life, initiate and maintain new relationships and activities, start taking care of yourself *physically* and *emotionally,* and detach yourself from the irresponsible and irrational behaviors of the drinker. You need to remember that consistency is the key to both helping yourself and the alcohol abuser in your life, consistency in each of these areas. Finally, it is important to begin these activities *today.* Begin the helping process today and not tomorrow. It is too easy to procrastinate for a few weeks, months, or never initiate the recovery process.

One of the most difficult barriers to helping irresponsible drinkers of all types is simply getting them to an appropriate counselor or treatment program. Today there are a diversity of treatments available for people who misuse alcohol. Furthermore, most of these treatments really are helpful, they do work! The same can be said of therapy and treatments for adult children of alcoholics and others who live with alcoholics or alcohol abusers. Individual counseling and psychotherapy, group therapy, marital or conjoint therapy, family therapy, educational films and classes, support groups, and such self-help groups as Alcoholics Anonymous, Al-Anon, Ala-Teen, and ACOA (Adult Children of Alcoholics) meetings are available on an outpatient basis for anyone with a drinking problem or anyone affected by the drinking behaviors of a parent, family member, or significant other. There are also a diversity of inpatient treatment programs available for alcohol abusers. These programs utilize all of the various treatment modalities listed earlier, but all professional services are provided on an inpatient basis. Thus, the alcohol abuser has several choices or options available if he or she needs inpatient care. Hospital based 21–30-day rehabilitation programs, intensive evening programs, detoxification centers, residential treatment centers, and halfway houses are treatment modalities that are available for people with alcohol use problems. These services are available in most communities throughout the United States.

If you happen to be living with an irresponsible drinker, the chances are high that *you* can benefit from counseling or some other form of treatment. Even if your spouse or loved one denies that he or she has a "drinking problem" and refuses to enter therapy or counseling, get help for yourself! There are many situations in which the drinker eventually decides to get help because his or her spouse or family member has gotten help and gotten better! You can help the drinker by helping yourself. Finally, you might need to remind yourself that it's simply okay to get help for yourself. It is not easy to live and survive with a problem drinker. Anyone who gets caught up in an extended close relationship with such an individual eventually becomes upset or psychologically conflicted. This is why alcoholism is commonly referred to as a "family disease."

SUMMARY

Learning influences and shapes every facet of human behavior. The belief that people can be taught to drink responsibly is based upon the premise that it is possible to consume ethanol in a responsible manner. People who do not manifest drinking problems have somehow learned to use ethanol in a non-problematic fashion.

Teaching and learning are also very complex processes. In spite of the hundreds of textbooks and thousands of scholarly research articles that have been published over several hundred years about every aspect of teaching and learning, surprisingly little has been written about the possibilities of teaching responsible alcohol use behaviors. In actuality, very little is known about the specifics of teaching and learning responsible alcohol use behaviors. Yet, the fact remains that millions and millions of people have successfully learned how *not* to drink abusively over the past several thousand years. It is logical to believe that they have been taught the various principals and techniques of responsible alcohol use by others as well as through different self-teaching, self-learning experiences.

There are many caveats associated with the matter of teaching responsible alcohol use behaviors. Nonetheless, several suggestions and guidelines for teaching responsible alcohol use behaviors were delineated in this chapter. These guidelines include: beginning at home, beginning early, being consistent, openly focusing on *all* issues associated with alcohol use, involving schools and the educational system in the process, utilizing all media resources and actively involving industry, all work environments, churches, and all state and federal government health agencies. The deterrents to teaching rational and responsible alcohol use behaviors were also touched upon in this chapter.

It was emphasized in this chapter that there are a diversity of different types of irresponsible drinkers. Furthermore, these individuals consume alcohol irresponsibly for a diversity of different reasons! Alcoholics cannot drink responsibly, because they have a physical disease that seems to preclude the possibility of long-term social or responsible consumption. Many secondary alcoholics and alcohol abusers drink irresponsibly in order to cope with any number of different problems and conflicts. Thus, the fact remains that millions of people either cannot or choose not to drink responsibly. They are irresponsible drinkers. According to *Webster's Dictionary,* the word irresponsible means "not required to answer to some higher authority (or power); not liable to be called into question; subject to no oversight or control; not based on sound reasoned considerations; uttered without regard to truth, propriety, or fairness; mentally inadequate to bear responsibility in an acceptable or normal manner; unprepared or unwilling to meet financial responsibilities." This definition describes the global drinking style of all "irresponsible drinkers."

The consequences of irresponsible alcohol use are all too often destructive and non-productive. As emphasized in this chapter, irresponsible drinkers as well as their spouses, families, and loved ones need help. Alcohol abusers are relatively different and unique individuals who need individualized treatments. Likewise, the people who live with irresponsible drinkers also need to be involved in treatments and rehabilitation programs that meet their individual needs. Several treatment alternatives for irresponsible drinkers and their families were discussed in this chapter. If there is an important person in your life who is an irresponsible drinker, get help and treatment for yourself and also make every effort to help the drinker get help—today!

Chapter 14

ALTERNATIVE PERSPECTIVES ON RESPONSIBLE DRINKING

INTRODUCTION

When I initially began to organize the content of this book, I began to realize how little I actually knew about the basic beliefs of several of my respected friends and colleagues in the addictions treatment field about the matter of responsible drinking. All of these behavioral scientists have been actively involved in the field of chemical dependency treatment for more than ten years. Their publications, lecturing and consultation work, dedication, and contributions to the field are monumental—they really are "experts" in the most real and accurate sense of the word! These realities made it absolutely imperative for me to include their ideas about responsible alcohol use in this book.

Thus, several months ago I personally corresponded with each of the contributors to this final chapter and asked that they candidly share their ideas and beliefs about the concept of responsible drinking. Their personal responses to this request form the *unedited* content of this chapter. Just as I found their ideas to be interesting and educational, I suggest that the reader will find the responses of each contributor to be very informative. Each contributor has candidly expressed his or her basic professional and personal viewpoint about responsible drinking. Several of the experts that I corresponded with declined the invitation to contribute to this chapter. In general, they felt that the subject matter or issue was still "too controversial" and "professionally too risky." I fully respect and sensitively appreciate their decisions.

Information about each contributor is provided before his or her discussion of responsible drinking. This information will help the reader more clearly appreciate each expert's academic background, clinical experience and orientation, and viewpoints as expressed in this chapter. The ideas and contributions of these behavioral scientists are clearly not ephemeral.

Thomas E. Bratter, Ed.D. Doctor Bratter is President of the John Dewey Academy in Great Barrington, Massachusetts. He is the author and/or editor of such books as **Alcoholism and Substance Abuse: Strategies for Clinical Intervention** (The Free Press, 1985) and **How To Survive Your Adolescent's Adolescence** (Little, Brown, 1984). Doctor Bratter is a psychotherapist who has been involved in the treatment of substance abusers and addicts for over twenty years. He has served on the editorial boards of numerous professional journals and is a regular contributor to these journals.

I am pleased to be given the opportunity to present my personal and professional views about the issue of "responsible drinking." Before addressing the myth of "responsible drinking," I think it is important to note that never have I, or any member of my family, experienced any drinking and/or drug problems. I have not had a drink for more than three years. I would estimate my total consumption of alcohol as I approach the half-century mark to be less than ten gallons. Professionally, for twenty-five years, I have worked primarily with adolescents (and their families) who have been addicted to alcohol and/or psychoactive substances. Vicariously, I have witnessed the agony of addiction which has raped individuals of their self-respect and productivity while concurrently ravaging their respective families who were reduced to impotent observers (and enablers). I see no glamour, no excitement, only potential monumental depression and self-destruction connected with drinking. I have devoted my professional life to helping individuals reclaim their existence from the no-win/no-exit labyrinth of alcoholism and addiction.

With no exceptions, I categorically believe the only realistic approach for individuals who previously have been dependent on or addicted to any psychoactive substance is abstinence. I subscribe to the simplistic brilliance of Alcoholics Anonymous' dictum, "Stay sober for twenty-four hours." Alcoholics Anonymous reduces the mandate of lifetime abstinence to a manageable "one day at a time."

Drinking responsibly or in moderation suggests that such behavior will not harm one's self or the welfare of others. I intend to prove this contention is false. There is no reputable scientific study that confirms that alcohol is a legitimate medicine or nutrient. Alcohol has no redeeming physiological, psychological, or social use. Societal economic costs are so staggering that drinking is indefensible. At least 10 percent of society escalates their "responsible drinking" to the point where they become addicted. How is it possible to term any activity "responsible" which produces such insidious results? I wish to pose the practical philosophical proposition, "Responsible to whom?" and systematically provide irrefutable responses. The answers are clear. The individual retains a primary responsibility to him or herself, family and friends, and to society.

Firstly, what is the impact of alcohol on the self? Pharmacologically, alcohol is toxic. There is physiological evidence that the ingestion of alcohol produces permanent damage to the basic unit of the body, i.e. the cell. The clinical data document that drinkers increase the chances of medical complications such as degenerative heart disease, digestive system malfunctions, arteriosclerosis, and cancer, etc. Alcohol adversely affects body organs such as heart, brain, liver, lungs, pancreas, etc. It is not known whether this damage occurs because drinking is cumulative or is dependent upon the amount ingested.

Alcohol is addictive. Detoxification from alcohol is a complicated and dangerous procedure which needs to be done with competent medical supervision in an inpatient setting. Detoxification occurs by gradually decreasing the dosage of alcohol consumption, because the by-product could be delirium tremens, which, in extreme cases, can cause cardiac arrest.

Alcohol is a mood-altering drug. For some, alcohol serves as a stimulant. Any consumption of alcohol increases the individual's assertiveness. The probability of a verbal argument and/or physical altercation, therefore, is increased directly in proportion to the amount of drinking. Sixty percent of all homicides have been traced directly to alcohol abuse. There is no way to estimate how many assaults have been provoked by excessive drinking. For others, alcohol can be a depressant. Sadly, but significantly, autopsies performed on suicide victims indicate that more than 50 percent were drinking or were inebriated when they killed themselves. More than 50 percent of all automobile fatalities are caused by drivers who have been drinking.

Secondly, what is the impact of alcohol on the family? Psychologically, the drinker implicitly communicates a noxious message to other family members. Any individual who drinks, even if the quantity remains insignificant, suggests there is some sort of dependence whether to calm the nerves, to escape from the pressures of daily life, and/or to feel good. To use a potent addictive psychoactive substance as the magic elixir of problems can create more serious ones than it resolves. Alcoholics have well-deserved reputations for being dishonest, manipulative and ego-centric. All experts agree that the impact of alcoholism can be devastating on children and adolescents. Adults who had an alcoholic parent(s) remain at risk decades after they started their own families. These adults have been unable to resolve many problems associated directly with their parents' drinking patterns which interferes with their abilities to be nurturing. It remains irrelevant whether the inter-generational tendency toward alcoholism is caused by heredity or is a learned response, because the degree of suffering is the same. Alcoholism is a devastating legacy to bestow on the young and innocent. Is it responsible behavior to indulge one's self when innocent others become contaminated?

Most terrifying is the recent scientific finding that some are born with a genetic predisposition to alcoholism. There is no way to identify those who are at risk of becoming so addicted. Recent surveys estimate that 30 percent of all sixth graders periodically drink which increases dramatically the number who will become problem drinkers.

Thirdly, what is the impact of alcohol on society? This, perhaps, is the esoteric question to answer because there are so many considerations. Alcohol always has been used to gain an unfair advantage. "Get the other drunk" and "Press for an advantage" is a common practice in business. How many contracts have been negotiated and signed when one of the parties was drunk? How many females have been seduced when they were drunk?

Etched in our consciousness by daily pictoral bombardment by television and the mass media is the rampant malnutrition and starvation in the world which affects 10 percent of the total population. Conveniently hidden from the public by the powerful, self-serving liquor lobby is the startling fact that more than one ton of corn or other grain produces only one gallon of ethanol, which is the primary ingredient of alcohol. This enormity of food waste is so criminally staggering that it defies comprehension. How many hundreds of thousands of people have starved to death because the food they desperately needed was diverted to making alcohol ought to be asked. Refusing to drink, if viewed from this perspective, is a powerful protest against world hunger and starvation.

How many car accidents have been caused by mechanics who were drinking when they made repairs, whose judgment was impaired? How many families suffer when someone is hurt or killed due to another's drinking? My guess is that less than 10 percent of all families are unaffected by alcohol abuse. No other epidemic in the history of the world, including the bubonic plague in the Middle Ages and the dreaded AIDS of the twentieth century, has been so devastating to so many.

It defies my sense of logic and decency how drinking any amount of alcohol, no matter how inconsequential, can be considered "responsible," because the potential for abuse and suffering is so great. Absolute abstinence from alcohol, therefore, is the only responsible action.

Chad D. Emrick, Ph.D. Doctor Emrick is a licensed Clinical Psychologist. He is respected throughout the United States and abroad as a researcher in the realm of outcome effectiveness of alcoholism treatments. Doctor Emrick has been involved in alcoholism research and treatment for over fifteen years. He has been a contributor to several alcohol textbooks and his research efforts have been published in such respected journals as **The American Psychologist** and **Journal of Alcohol Studies.**

Basically, I view "responsible drinking" as that which does not lead to problems for the drinker or others. From a macro perspective this refers to drinking in such a manner that the drinker does not encounter marital problems, work difficulties, health problems, legal troubles and the like. From a more micro perspective, such a definition refers to drinking that does not impair health maintenance activities, family and social relationships, constructive hobbies, spiritual/philosophical pursuits and so forth. If, for example, an individual's habit is to have one or two drinks at home after a day's work and such drinking leads to a "shutting down" with the result that family members are neglected, physical exercise is not done, hobbies lie fallow, and philosophical/spiritual pursuits are left unattended, then the individual is not drinking "responsibly." Responsible drinking places alcohol use in the periphery of life. If drinking occupies a more central place, it is my opinion that the drinker does best to remove alcohol completely from his/her life in order to "force" attention to other, more important aspects of living.

William Glasser, M.D. Doctor Glasser is a Psychiatrist and Founder of the Reality Therapy Institute. Doctor Glasser is recognized through-

> out the world as the innovator of Reality Therapy. He is the author of such books as **Reality Therapy** (Harper and Row, 1965), **Schools Without Failure** (Harper and Row, 1969), **Positive Addiction** (Harper and Row, 1976), and **Take Effective Control of Your Life** (Harper and Row, 1984). His creative as well as pragmatic contributions to the fields of mental health and addictions treatment are monumental.

Before we can talk about responsible drinking, I think we have to define the word responsibility. This is a word that I, as a Reality Therapist, have given a great deal of thought to. It is a therapy which advocates responsible living and taking responsibility for one's actions. To me, responsible people are those who can satisfy their needs in a way that does not impair their life. This means, a way that does not impair their ability to work, socialize or play, and, at the same time, does not impair the ability of anyone else to satisfy his or her needs in the same responsible way. Since all behavior is always our best attempt to satisfy our needs at the time, then drinking alcohol would be, of course, a behavior that attempts to do the same. If people in their attempts to satisfy their needs through alcohol produce any impairment in their lives or in the lives of others, then this would not be responsible drinking. Therefore, a responsible drinker would be a person who can drink and feel as if one or more of his or her needs are satisfied through drinking, and yet do so in a way that does not impair his or her life or the lives of other people.

This would be the same definition for a responsible driver, a responsible eater, a responsible worker, a responsible husband, wife or child, teacher, or anyone else engaged in any other activity whatsoever. The only reason one would define responsible drinking is that many drinkers are not responsible. They drink, and with alcohol they get the feeling that their needs are satisfied, but at the same time it becomes apparent to others, and eventually to them, that what they are doing is impairing their lives or the lives of others, even though at the time they believe that they are satisfying their needs. These are not responsible drinkers, and if this occurs, then it is not responsible drinking.

Beyond these definitions, I really don't think I can add very much to what most people believe is responsible drinking. I know very few alcoholics, actually no drinking alcoholics at the present time; yet, I know a great many people who drink responsibly and enjoy their drinking, feel that it satisfies their needs to some extent, and who are totally unimpaired by the process and certainly don't impair anyone else. Like responsible drivers, responsible parents, responsible businessmen, these people are not news. They don't produce problems, there are no books written about them, and probably there's no need to write extensively about them. Nevertheless, I think the idea of this book, to write a little more about them, is wise.

Perhaps, what needs most to be kept in mind is that when a person is attempting to use an addicting drug like alcohol, it's very easy to slip from responsible to irresponsible. A responsible drinker can see this coming and can therefore abort the process. An irresponsible drinker may or may not see it coming, but whether or not he or she does, he or she has no desire to abort the process. If a responsible drinker finds that this is becoming increasingly difficult, then a responsible drinker will turn into a responsible abstainer. Some people don't have the strength to drink responsibly. They are responsible enough to realize they can't drink responsibly, and for these people, their only possibility is to abstain from alcohol. To help them do that, I personally advise that they look into the AA program, even though they may never become alcoholic. They say to themselves, I've never been an active alcoholic, but I have the possibility of becoming one and I'd like to join AA because I think that would help me in a life of abstaining from alcohol.

Terence T. Gorski, M.A., CAC. Terry Gorski is the President of The Cenaps Corporation. His contributions to the alcoholism treatment field span a period of over 15 years. Terry's contributions in the realm of relapse prevention are recognized throughout the United States. He is the author of such books as **Staying Sober: A Guide to Relapse Prevention** (Independence Press, 1986) and **Counseling for Relapse Prevention** (Independence Press, 1982).

As you are obviously aware, the controlled drinking and responsible drinking issues are quite controversial.

The problems that people experience related to alcohol use fall on a continuum. At the far end of the continuum are people who use alcohol in low quantities, infrequently and with no discernible repetitive patterns.

These people by definition experience no problems with alcohol. These are the people whom I would define as social, non-dependent, non-problem drinkers. These individuals are in the minority. The people who are social, non-dependent, non-problem drinkers use alcohol as they would any other beverage. They are not consuming alcohol for its drug-like properties.

The majority of drinkers in America consume alcohol in a dependent fashion. For the purpose of this discussion we will call it psychosocial dependency. A person is psycho-socially dependent upon alcohol when they require the effects of alcohol in order to comfortably complete one or more life tasks. Most American drinkers are dependent upon the effects of alcohol to assist them in one or more tasks of their life. A large number of these drinkers are dependent in very narrow areas. A gynecologist once reported that the average patient that he treated conceived a baby on Friday night at half-past eleven after 2.3 martinis. What this implies is that many American adults are dependent upon the effects of alcohol to enhance sexuality. They are psychosocially dependent. This dependency, however, does not progress and it does not create a problem.

The level of dependency can vary from mild to severe. A person who is mildly dependent is able to function normally in all areas without the alcohol, but they perceive some level of discomfort when doing so. A moderately dependent person is able to perform most functions in life without alcohol, but at times they are so uncomfortable that they choose to avoid the activities that they depend on alcohol to comfortably complete. The severely dependent person is the person who is incapable of functioning normally in one or more life areas without the effects of alcohol to assist him in functioning.

This psychosocial dependency is often defined as social drinking. I don't believe that it is. These individuals are in high risk of becoming problematic in their use patterns or developing an addictive disease.

Other users do develop problems. They are what is classically called alcohol abusers or problem drinkers. These persons experience adverse consequences as a result of their alcohol and drug use. Some people experience isolated episodes or sporadic periods of problematic drinking. For others the problems are chronic and at times progressive. Some of these problem drinkers are physically dependent upon alcohol, in that they exhibit tolerance in withdrawal. Others are not.

The final category are people who develop physical tolerance and dependence upon alcohol. In other words they become physically addicted. Some people who are physically addicted develop problematic behaviors as a consequence. Others do not. There are some addicted people who are able to use maintenance doses of alcohol without any observable psychosocial effects while using. The only reason they continue to use is because the short-term and long-term withdrawal makes them uncomfortable or dysfunctional when they attempt to stop.

I, therefore, define responsible or social drinking as any pattern of alcohol and drug use that does not create psychosocial dependency, problematic consequences, or physical dependency.

The guidelines for this would be to define a safe level of alcohol use. Three factors need to be considered: quantity, frequency, and consequence.

Anyone who has problematic consequences as a result of any drinking episode is not a responsible drinker. Responsible drinkers rarely do things while drinking that they regret later.

In terms of quantity, most responsible drinkers do not drink beyond the point of mild mood alteration. Responsible drinkers rarely become intoxicated. If they do become intoxicated, they know in advance that they are going to drink to intoxication and take steps to protect themselves. For a responsible drinker episodes of drinking to the point of intoxication occur once per year or less. Anyone who becomes intoxicated more than once per year, in my opinion, is not a responsible drinker. The reason is that more frequent intoxication leads to physiological and neurological damage.

A responsible drinker does not consume alcohol in quantities sufficient to produce noticeable mood alteration on a regular basis. Anyone who drinks to the point of mood alteration more frequently than twice per week will become psychosocially dependent upon the mood-altering effect of alcohol to cope with the task they are drinking while participating in. It is impossible to consistently engage in social, recreational, or family activities in an alcohol-altered state without becoming dependent upon it. There is ample evidence in this in the state dependent memory literature. There is a very fine book on the subject called, *Alcohol and Human Memory*.

The key question that needs to be answered to determine responsible drinking is how much is too much. There is a very fine book on this subject by Leonard Gross, published by Balantine Press in 1983. Mr. Gross is a journalist who is a heavy social drinker who became concerned about the consequences of his own drinking. He did journalistic research into the question of how much alcohol was harmful. I would like to share with you some of the conclusions which were presented in his book.

"It makes sense that there is a threshold below which one can drink with a measure of confidence and above which the danger increases. But it also makes sense that this threshold is not the line it has been depicted as being but, rather, a flexible space that shrinks or widens dependent upon individual susceptibilities and the nature of each disease."

In other words there is no universal safe level of alcohol consumption. There is no one norm against which everyone can judge themselves. People who are highly susceptible to damage in addiction to alcohol will experience harmful consequences and thus become irresponsible drinkers at very low levels of alcohol consumption. Other people can drink more frequently in larger amounts without still exhibiting a responsible pattern of use. Anyone who has a genetic family history of alcoholism is irresponsible if they drink on any regular and consistent basis.

It is obvious that the chances of a long and healthy life go down beyond a certain point in direct proportion to the amount that one drinks. Social drinkers who imbibe three to five drinks a day are at greater risk of an early death than those who imbibe one or two, and those who drink six or more drinks a day are at greater risk yet. The mortality tables confirm this.

In other words, my recommendation would be that a maximum cutoff for social drinking would be two to three normal-sized drinks per day, but even that limit may be dangerous for people who are predisposed genetically to alcoholism.

It is also obvious that heavy drinkers do not develop serious alcohol and drug-related problems until late in life. They appear to drink with immunity and hence responsibly in their younger days. But they pay a heavy toll later in life. Therefore, any pattern of heavy consumption, regardless of short-term consequences, should be regarded as irresponsible due to the long-term effects. Nathaniel Brandon, in his book, *The Psychology of Self Esteem*, defines a mentally healthy person as "one that plans for their physical, psychological, and social well-being for the long-term of their life." A person who drinks abusively in their teens, twenties, and thirties does not meet this definition. They are definitely setting the stage for adverse health problems and psychosocial problems later in life.

When talking about responsible drinking, it is important to divide problems related to alcohol into two categories: first, those experienced by the person with alcoholism or addictive disease; second, routine health problems that are exacerbated by the apparently responsible use of alcohol. People who have hypertension, diabetes, or heart disease and continue to use alcohol are placing their health in jeopardy even though they may never develop symptoms of alcoholism. These people are not responsible drinkers.

I would strongly recommend that you review Chapter 10 in the book, *How Much is Too Much,* by Leonard Gross for more detailed discussion.

My own personal views can be summarized as this:

(1) Any person who uses alcohol consistently to the point of mood alteration is not a responsible drinker. A responsible drinker is a person who uses alcohol as a beverage and stops intake of alcohol at the first signs of mood alteration.

(2) Any person who drinks on a regular basis to the point of mood alteration will develop a level of psychosocial dependency. A person with mild levels of psychosocial dependency may be considered a responsible drinker but, as soon as the person becomes significantly uncomfortable with one or more life tasks that need to be performed without the assistance of the mood-altering effects of alcohol, can be said to be irresponsible. Any person who develops the need for alcohol use in order to cope comfortably with life tasks, in my mind, is not a responsible drinker. Why? Because in the absence of alcohol they will be unable to competently manage these tasks of their life.

(3) Any person who imbibes more frequently than three times per week and consumes more than three normal-sized drinks in my mind is considered an irresponsible drinker. The reason is that there is significant biomedical evidence that even if these people do not develop alcoholism, they will be damaging their health in the long run. They will pay a heavy price for their heavy use.

(4) Anyone who experiences problems in their life either physically, psychologically, or socially due to their drinking is not a responsible drinker. If a person has problems and continues to drink in spite of their problems, they are either unaware of the cause-effect relationship between the alcohol and their problems, or they have emotional problems that prevent them from taking adequate self-care, or they are addicted and, due to the addiction, they are out of control of their judgment and behavior. These people cannot be

said to be responsible, because they cannot be said to be in rational control of their ability to act in their own best interest.

Conway Hunter, Jr., M.D. Doctor Hunter is a physician and alcoholism consultant who is recognized throughout the world for his contributions to the addictions treatment field. He has lectured and provided consultation services in the areas of alcoholism and substance abuse throughout the U.S. and abroad for twenty years. Doctor Hunter has influenced the development of numerous addiction treatment facilities throughout the Southeast. He has also published in the field of alcoholism literature.

Careful consideration must be given to an appraisal of the phenomenon of "responsible drinking." If we were to define responsibility as "the ability to respond," then we must look at how alcohol affects one's ability to respond. It has been clearly proven that very small amounts of alcohol will cause some degree of motor and cognitive depression. Certainly no one will disagree that alcohol in any form is a central nervous system depressant and, therefore, will diminish one's ability to respond. In fact, we must then categorize responsible drinking as depression or sedation in social interactions.

This is not to say that there isn't a place for alcohol on social occasions. Ever since man discovered wine, alcohol has been used as a facilitator of conviviality—or, if you will, a social lubricant. There are, of course, occasions where the sedative tranquilizing effects of alcohol may be beneficial, and certainly small amounts of this drug can be considered relatively harmless to most people. There are some who must never use alcohol: those who have no tolerance for the drug, or the 12 percent or so who are or will become alcoholics. (There is no need to go into alcoholism or genetics here, but there are those predisposed through physiological and environmental factors, and for them there is no responsible or social drinking.)

This is not intended to moralize or condemn the use of alcohol but to pose to the objective intellectual the question, "Does alcohol actually produce any benefit to anyone? Or does the negative potential outweigh the value of its use?" Society will continue to use sedative hypnotic agents to alter reality, and when drugs of this nature become socially acceptable, they then are adapted into the structure of society. During the last two decades, we have seen the social acceptance of marijuana and cocaine. But as always, the social choice of most Americans remains alcohol.

> ***Judy Rainforth-McGlynn, M.S.*** Judy was the first Program Director of the Family Recovery Center in Grand Island, Nebraska. She developed and managed this program for several years before becoming the Director of Treatment at the Genesis Program in California. Her contributions to the field of addictions treatment and program development are recognized throughout the Midwest. Judy is a close friend of Claudia Black, MSW, Ph.D., and she is sensitive to the needs of adult children of alcoholics and families of substance abusers.

Most of us, prior to taking off on a long auto journey, have our cars checked. We want to make sure that the important parts—tires, brakes, engine—are safe and okay. Before takeoff, commercial jet crews go through an intense and complete safety checklist. Would it not make as much sense to go through a safety checklist before we embark on a lifetime journey of being a "social drinker?"

It seems to me that to be a "responsible drinker" we need to make a responsible decision. To make a responsible decision we have to have some facts. After gathering the facts and weighing the risks and benefits, we can make a responsible choice to be a responsible drinker—one whom is responsible for that decision to drink and all that goes with that decision.

We need some suggestions on what we will want on our drinking list. Here are my suggestions:

Start with your immediate family—your family of origin. Is there a family history of alcoholism or addiction to mood-altering drugs? If so, then you should carefully weigh the strong possibility that you could become addicted if you choose to drink.

Next, carefully look at your present and past mental health patterns. If you have excessive bouts with depression, free-floating anxieties, or paranoia, then the use of alcohol could compound these problems. In the absence of medical causes, fluctuations in sleeping patterns, energy levels, and body weight can be further complicated by your use of alcohol. Any such symptoms should be carefully weighed against any possible benefits of alcohol.

Alcohol is a potent mood-altering drug. It is a foreign substance in the body. It is an irritant to sensitive tissues and damaging to vital organs, even at low dosage levels.

Review your personal medical history. If you have problems in your digestive tract—stomach, intestines, pancreas—alcohol will not make the situation better.

We have heard what alcohol can do to the liver, but alcohol can be just as damaging to our cardiovascular system, especially the heart.

Recently published studies seem to warn us of the potential "cause-and-effect" relationship between even moderate amounts of alcohol consumption and various female cancers. Alcohol passes through the placenta, bringing the potent chemical to the unborn baby. Published studies clearly warn expectant mothers to refrain from drinking alcohol.

Alcohol impairs us mentally and physically. Studies indicate this happening at very moderate levels of consumption. They are the basis for recommending that states adopt new levels for determining whether someone is drunk and driving. Currently, most states use blood alcohol levels of .10 percent.

If you decide to become a "responsible drinker," then commit yourself to an annual drinking checkup. Do this checkup with either two other family members or two other significant people in your life. Questions should include the following:

(1) Are you a "different person" after only a couple of drinks?
(2) Are you drinking more, say, from a glass of wine twice a week to one glass every evening?
(3) Are you drinking to numb feelings of pain, sorrow, sadness or anger? Do you drink to enhance joy and periodic success or accomplishment? Has your drinking ever caused you embarrassment, or caused you to injure someone, or caused damage to property? These questions are not inclusive but a place to start.

I believe that everytime we find ourselves in a situation where we must decide whether to have an alcoholic drink or not, we should do a quick inventory of ourselves and our past. I believe that if we choose to drink socially, we annually submit to a drinking pattern inventory.

By following this process, you may be able to remain a social and responsible drinker. Remember, no alcoholic ever purposely set out to become one. Most thought they too were nothing more than sociable, responsible drinkers.

SUMMARY

The viewpoints that were expressed in this chapter reflect a diversity of perceptions and beliefs about responsible alcohol use. Indeed, so-called "experts" in the fields of mental health and chemical dependency treatment seem to manifest divergent opinions about responsible drinking that mirror the beliefs of the general public. Doctor Bratter indicates that any use of alcohol is irresponsible, while Doctor Glasser and Doctor Emrick indicate that there are relatively distinct parameters of responsible alcohol use. Judy Rainforth-McGlynn wisely suggests that all drinkers need to periodically evaluate the "responsible-irresponsible" dimensions of their alcohol use. All of the contributors to this chapter realize that drinking ethanol may result in alcohol abuse or alcoholism for some people.

It is my hope that the reader will use the information and concepts that were emphasized throughout the book. You can be more aware and more objective about the responsible-irresponsible aspects of your own alcohol use as well as the drinking behaviors of your friends or family members. If you do choose to imbibe, apply the guidelines that are delineated in this book to help *you* drink responsibly. Apply these guidelines at parties, social functions, and with colleagues so that you might reinforce their responsible choices about alcohol use. Perhaps you will be able to use the information in this book to influence an irresponsible drinker in your life to stop drinking or seek professional help for his or her alcohol abuse.

Finally, it is important to remember that it is always responsible and *socially appropriate* to choose not to drink, in any context! If you do drink, drink responsibly; if you can't drink responsibly, don't drink.

When you find yourself feeling confused about entertaining with alcohol, driving after drinking, drinking in the presence of your children, or any of the other topics of this book, take some time and reread the chapters that apply to your particular dilemma or situation. We all need to rethink or reconsider these issues from time to time!

REFERENCES AND SUGGESTED READINGS

Bales, R. F.: Cultural differences in rates of alcoholism. *Quat. J. Stud. Alc.*, *6*:480–499, 1946.

Black, C.: *It Will Never Happen To Me.* Denver: MAC Publishers, 1981.

Bratter, T. E.: Special clinical psychotherapeutic concerns for alcoholic and drug-addicted individuals. In T. E. Bratter and G. G. Forrest (Eds.), *Alcoholism and Substance Abuse: Strategies for Clinical Intervention.* New York: Free Press, 1985.

Bratter, T. E., and Forrest, G. G. (Eds.): *Alcoholism and Substance Abuse: Strategies for Clinical Intervention.* New York: Free Press, 1985.

Eysenck, H. J.: *The Effects of Psychotherapy.* New York: International Science Press, 1966.

Forrest, G. G.: *The Diagnosis and Treatment of Alcoholism.* Springfield: Charles C Thomas, 1978.

Forrest, G. G.: *Alcoholism, Narcissism and Psychopathology.* Springfield: Charles C Thomas, 1983.

Forrest, G. G.: *Alcoholism and Human Sexuality.* Springfield: Charles C Thomas, 1983.

Forrest, G. G.: *Intensive Psychotherapy of Alcoholism.* Springfield: Charles C Thomas, 1984.

Forrest, G. G.: *How to Cope with a Teenage Drinker: New Alternatives and Hope for Parents and Families.* New York: Fawcett Crest, 1984.

Forrest, G. G.: *How to Live with a Problem Drinker and Survive.* New York: Atheneum, 1986.

Glasser, W.: *Reality Therapy.* New York: Harper and Row, 1964.

Glasser, W.: *Positive Addiction.* New York: Harper and Row, 1976.

Hughes, C. H.: Moral (affective) insanity—psychosensory insanity (1834). In M. H. Stone (Ed.): *Essential Papers on Borderline Disorders: One Hundred Years at the Border.* New York: New York University Press, 1986.

Heath, D. B.: Addiction. In E. Gottheil, K. A. Pouley, T. E. Skoloda, and H. M. Waxman (Eds.): *Etiologic Aspects of Alcohol and Drug Abuse.* Springfield: Charles C Thomas, 1983.

Milt, H.: *Basic Handbook for Alcoholism.* New Jersey: Scientific Aids Publications, 1969.

Mulford, H. A.: Drinking and Deviant Behavior, U.S.A., 1963. *Quat. J. Stud. Alc.*, *25*:634–650, 1964.

Mumey, J.: *Loving an Alcoholic: Help and Hope for Significant Others.* Chicago: Contemporary Books, 1985.

Mumey, J.: *The Joy of Being S.O.B.E.R.* Chicago: Contemporary Books, 1984.
Mumey, J.: *Young Alcoholics.* Chicago: Contemporary Books, 1986.
Mowrer, O. H.: *The Crisis in Psychiatry and Religion.* Princeton: Van Nostrand, 1961.
Mowrer, O. H.: *The New Group Therapy.* Princeton: Van Nostrand, 1964.
Orford, J.: *Excessive Appetites: A Psychological View of Addictions.* New York: John Wiley, 1985.
Pace, N. A., and Cross, W.: *Guidelines to Safe Drinking.* New York: Fawcett Crest, 1984.
Stone, M. H. (Ed.): *Essential Papers on Borderline Disorders: One Hundred Years at the Border.* New York: New York University Press, 1986.
Timkin, D.: Assessment and Treatment of High Risk DUI Offenders. Lecture presented at Psychotherapy Associates, P.C. 13th International Advanced Winter Symposium, "Treatment of Addictive Disorders," Antlers Plaza Hotel, Colorado Springs, Colorado, February 4, 1987.
Wallace, J.: *Alcoholism: New Light on the Disease.* Newport: Edgehill Newport Publications, 1985.
Wayne, G. H.: *Minority Alcoholism: Myths vs. Research.* Colorado Springs: Aspen Educational Consulting, 1984.
Weigscheider-Cruse, S.: *Another Chance: Hope and Health for the Alcoholic Family.* Palo Alto: Science and Behavior Books, 1981.
Webster's 9th New Collegiate Dictionary: Springfield: G. & C. Merriam, 1985.
NIAAA: *The Young Drinkers: Teenagers and Alcohol.* Pompano Beach: Health Communications, 1978.
Woititz, J. G.: *Adult Children of Alcoholics.* Pompano Beach: Health Communications, 1983.

INDEX